English Te

Copyright

Published by Azhar ul Haque Sario
azhar.sario@hotmail.co.uk

Table of Contents

Foreword

Hello and welcome to "English Tenses!" It's perfect for anyone who wants to get better at English grammar, especially the part about tenses.

Think of this book as your friendly guide through the world of English tenses. We start with the basics, which is really important. You'll get to know each tense step by step. First, we talk about the simple present tense — it's the one we use for things we do all the time or things that are always true. After that, we'll explore more tricky tenses like the future perfect continuous tense. This one is for talking about things that will keep going until a certain time in the future.

The best part about this book? It's written in super simple English. We know that learning about tenses can be tough, especially if English isn't your first language. So, we've made sure everything is easy and clear.

Each chapter is more than just explanations. They show you how to use each tense in real life, with examples and exercises for you to try. This makes it a great book for everyone — whether you're a student, teacher, working professional, or just curious about English grammar. "English Tenses" is your complete, friendly guide to really understanding English tenses.

So, come along on this fun learning adventure. You'll see how precise and beautiful English tenses can be, and it'll make talking and writing in English easier, whether it's for chatting with friends or for work.

Happy reading, and enjoy your learning journey!

Chapter 1: Introduction to English Tenses

Tenses in English grammar are the backbone of communication. They give life to our words, painting the time of action with clarity. Like an artist choosing colors to bring a scene to life, we select different tenses to illustrate when an event takes place. Imagine for a moment a world without the concept of time in language. It would be a canvas with no distinction between the sunrise of yesterday, the noon of today, and the twilight of tomorrow. Tenses allow us to avoid such confusion by providing a temporal context to our words.

In the simplest terms, tenses are a way to travel in time using language. They take us back to past events, anchor us in the present moment, or propel us into the future. There are three main time frames—past, present, and future—and each has four aspects: simple, continuous, perfect, and perfect continuous. These aspects give us a detailed sense of time, like different brushes that add texture and depth to the story we're telling.

The importance of tenses cannot be overstated. They help us share our histories, express our current feelings, and voice our future dreams. Without them, our stories would be incomplete, our instructions confusing, and our promises hollow. Tenses also let us build a narrative, establish cause and effect, and maintain coherence in our communication. They are the difference between "I eat," "I am eating," "I ate," and "I will eat," each a different shade of meaning.

Tenses are not just about when; they are also about how long and how often. This is where the aspects come into play. The simple aspect is like a single snapshot, a moment captured and frozen in time. The continuous aspect is like a video, showing an action in motion. The perfect aspect is the photo album that emphasizes the completion of an event, and the perfect continuous aspect is the long movie, illustrating an action that has been going on for a while and may still be ongoing.

Rarely discussed, but equally important, is the role tenses play in politeness and social context. The choice between "Could you please close the window?" and "Can you close the window?"

In technical terms, tenses are not only about verbs. They include modal verbs, auxiliary verbs, and sometimes nouns and adjectives. For example, "yesterday" is a past tense time indicator, while "soon" can imply future tense. These words help to fine-tune the temporal accuracy of our sentences.

The practical applications of tenses are endless. They are crucial in business communication, where clarity about timelines is vital. In law, the tense used in a contract can be the difference between an obligation and an option. In storytelling, tenses are the threads that weave together the tapestry of plot, setting, and character development.

To explore this further, consider how historians rely on tenses to frame events in context, or how a doctor might use tenses to understand a patient's medical history. Each profession uses tenses to add precision and clarity to their specific domains.

Lastly, to foster creativity, tenses can be played with, giving rise to complex storytelling techniques such as flashbacks or foreshadowing. A writer might use the present tense to lend immediacy to a story that took place in the past, or a future tense to create a sense of anticipation.

In conclusion, tenses are not just grammatical rules; they are the essential gears of language that enable the machinery of communication to function smoothly. They bring order to our thoughts, allow us to share experiences with accuracy, and let us engage with each other across time. Their mastery can lead to powerful expression, and their misuse can lead to equally powerful confusion. Understanding and using tenses is therefore not just a skill but an art, one that illuminates the timeline of our lives with precision and color.

The tapestry of English language is rich and complex, yet it is woven with some very fundamental threads. Among the most critical are the tenses, specifically the three main ones: past, present, and future. Each of these tenses offers us a unique way to express the timing of an action or a state of being, serving as a temporal beacon to our listeners or readers.

Let's embark on an explorative journey through these tenses, beginning with the past tense. When we talk about the past, we reach back into the memory vaults of time. The past tense is the guardian of history, of narratives long concluded, of actions that have been completed before now. It whispers to us tales of yesteryear, of moments that have danced away with the ticking clock. Whether it's a story of ancient empires, a recollection of a first birthday party, or a simple statement like "I walked," the past tense serves as our linguistic time machine.

In the realm of grammar, the past tense can be simple, as in "I walked," where the action is completed and there are no frills attached. But the past also has its complexities. The past continuous tense, for example, introduces a sense of an action in motion in the past, as in "I was walking." It paints a picture of a scene in progress, a snapshot of activity amid the river of time. Then there's the past perfect tense, which is a bit like a play within a play, showing us an action that was completed before another action in the past, as in "I had walked." And let's not forget the past perfect continuous, which might say, "I had been walking," implying an action that had been ongoing over a period in the past before another past event.

Shifting to the present tense, we find ourselves grounded in the moment. The present tense is the beating heart of language, the 'now' where we live and speak. "I walk" is the present simple, an action that is current, habitual, or a universal truth. Then, with a flicker of continuity, we have the present continuous: "I am walking," which signifies action at the moment of speaking. It's the difference between a static photo and a live broadcast. For actions that have a bearing on the present because they've just been completed, we use the present perfect tense: "I have walked." And when that action has been happening up until now and might continue, we employ the present perfect continuous: "I have been walking."

The future tense, on the other hand, opens the door to infinite possibilities. It speaks of events yet to come, plans laid out for the times ahead, dreams waiting to unfurl their wings. "I will walk" is the future simple, a declaration of what is to be. With the future continuous tense, "I will be walking," we anticipate an action in progress at a specific time in the future, as if marking a spot on a timeline. Then there's the future perfect tense, "I will have walked," which is used to say that an action will be completed by a certain future moment. And for actions that will continue up until a point in the future, we use the future perfect continuous: "I will have been walking."

But why are these tenses so crucial? The practical applications are myriad. Imagine programming a computer system, crafting a legal document, or setting a meeting agenda without a clear indication of time—it would be like trying to navigate without a compass. The tense you choose sets the stage for the expectation, the reality, and the retrospection of every action and decision.

Technically, the tenses are not standalone entities. They conspire with other words to give full color to their meaning. Adverbs of time like "yesterday," "now," and "tomorrow," modal verbs like "can" and "must," and other auxiliary verbs like "have" and "will," all play a role in shaping the tense.

The rarity in this knowledge lies not in the tenses themselves but in their mastery. To wield them effectively requires a keen sense of context, a deep understanding of nuance, and the ability to foresee how a sentence will land in the ears or eyes of the beholder.

To conclude, the past, present, and future tenses are not just grammatical constructs; they are the essence of storytelling, the currency of planners and historians, and the lifeblood of effective communication. They allow us to reminisce, to proclaim, to instruct, and to dream. Mastery of these tenses is akin to a musician mastering scales: the basics are essential, but the true art lies in how creatively and accurately one can play with them.

Tenses in the English language are like the framework of a building, each part with its unique role, ensuring that our verbal and written communication stands tall and clear. When we talk about tenses, we are referring to the way in which a verb changes to show when an action happens. There are three primary times when an action can take place: the past, the present, or the future. Each of these time frames is the foundation for the three basic tenses: past, present, and future.

The present tense, as straightforward as the hands of a clock at noon, represents actions that are currently ongoing or habitual. It is the tense of here and now. For instance, when we say, "I eat," we are using the simple present tense. It's akin to a snapshot, capturing an action in the moment or a habitual routine.

The past tense, on the other hand, is like a memory, a reflection of something that has already happened. When we talk about actions completed in the past, we typically add an

-ed to the end of regular verbs. For example, "I walked" tells us that the action of walking happened before now.

The future tense, with its forward-looking eye, talks about actions that have yet to happen. It's like a promise or a prediction, and in English, it's often formed with the help of the auxiliary verb "will." If we say, "I will write," we are casting our verb into the realm of what is to come.

Now, if we delve deeper, we find that each of these three tenses has four aspects: simple, continuous (also known as progressive), perfect, and perfect continuous. These aspects tell us more about the time of the action or state of being.

The simple aspect, used for general statements of fact or habits, is just as its name implies - uncomplicated. The continuous aspect adds a layer, indicating an action that is, was, or will be in progress. The perfect aspect steps in to represent an action that has been completed at a certain point in time, while the perfect continuous aspect blends the continuous and perfect aspects to show an action that began in the past and is still going on or has just finished.

Now, let's explore each tense and aspect with a little more detail and creativity:

Present Simple: The reliable storyteller of everyday routines. It narrates habits, general truths, and timeless facts like, "The sun rises in the East."

Present Continuous: This is the lens zooming in on actions happening right now. When we say, "I am reading," it's like watching a movie in real-time.

Present Perfect: Think of it as the bridge between past and present. It accounts for experiences or actions that have occurred at an unspecified time before now, as in "I have traveled to Spain."

Present Perfect Continuous: Here we have the storyteller of ongoing actions that began in the past and are still marching on or have just ceased, like footprints that are fresh on the ground. An example would be, "I have been studying for hours."

Past Simple: The history book of tenses. It tells tales of completed actions, such as "Shakespeare wrote plays."

Past Continuous: This aspect spins a yarn about past actions that were interrupted by other events or actions, akin to a play with a surprise intermission. For example, "I was walking when it started to rain."

Past Perfect: It's the deep memory, talking about an action that was completed before another action in the past took place. It's like looking at an old photograph before a more recent event.

Past Perfect Continuous: This is the past of the past, highlighting an ongoing action that was happening before another past action. It's the echo of footsteps that were heard even before the last ones, as in "I had been walking for hours before I finally stopped."

Future Simple: The crystal ball of tenses. It predicts or promises future actions. "I will learn to play the piano," promises an upcoming effort.

Future Continuous: Here we focus on actions that will be in progress at a certain point in the future, like a preview of what's to come.

Future Perfect: This tense tells us that by a certain time in the future, an action will have been completed. It's like marking a deadline on a calendar.

Future Perfect Continuous: The marathon runner of tenses, it speaks of an action that will continue up until a point in the future. "By the time you arrive, I will have been cooking for hours."

To truly grasp these tenses, one must not only understand but also practice them. Let's put our knowledge into action with some sample exercises:

Exercise 1: Identify the tense and aspect of the following sentences.

She writes in her journal every day.
They were watching TV when I called.
Will you have finished the report by tomorrow?
Answers:

Present Simple
Past Continuous
Present Perfect Continuous
Future Perfect
Exercise 2: Construct sentences using the prompts given.

Present Continuous (you / to read)
Past Perfect (they / to eat / dinner)
Future Simple (I / to visit / my grandparents)
Present Perfect (it / to snow)
Answers:

You are reading.
They had eaten dinner.
I will visit my grandparents.
It has snowed.
Understanding the basic structure of tenses equips us with the ability to narrate the past, articulate the present, and envision the future, thus unlocking the full spectrum of time in our language.

Understanding the concept of tenses in the English language is critical because they allow us to express the timing of actions, events, or states relative to the present moment. However, many learners and even fluent speakers harbor misconceptions about tenses that can lead to confusion and errors in communication. Let's explore some of these misconceptions and provide clarity on each.

Misconception 1: The Future Tense Always Requires "Will" or "Shall"
Many believe that to talk about the future, one must use "will" or "shall." While these are common ways to form the future tense, there are other methods. For instance, the present continuous tense is often used to describe a planned future event, and the present simple can be used for scheduled events, such as a bus departure.

Example Exercise:

Incorrect: I will meet you at the bus station tomorrow at eight because it is our schedule.
Correct: I am meeting you at the bus station tomorrow at eight because it is our schedule.
Solution:
The correct sentence uses the present continuous tense to convey a planned action in the future.

Misconception 2: The Present Perfect Tense is the Same as the Simple Past Tense
The present perfect tense (have/has + past participle) is sometimes used interchangeably with the simple past tense. This is incorrect as the present perfect connects the past action with the present, often to express experience, change, or a continued action, whereas the simple past refers to a specific point in time that is already over.

Example Exercise:

Incorrect: I saw that movie last month.
Correct: I have seen that movie.
Solution:
If the speaker's intention is to express an experience up to the present, "I have seen that movie" is the appropriate

choice. The use of "saw" implies the action is completely in the past with no connection to the present.

Misconception 3: Past Continuous Tense is Only Used for Interrupted Actions
It is a common belief that the past continuous tense (was/were + verb-ing) is used only to describe actions that were interrupted by another action. While this is a frequent use, the past continuous can also set the scene or describe parallel actions happening simultaneously in the past.

Example Exercise:

Incorrect: While I read a book, I listened to music.
Correct: While I was reading a book, I was listening to music.
Solution:
The correct sentence uses the past continuous tense to indicate that two continuous past actions were happening at the same time.

Misconception 4: "Used to" and "Would" Are Always Interchangeable When Talking About Past Habits
While both "used to" and "would" can refer to past habits, "would" is not used to describe states or situations that were true in the past. "Used to" can describe both states and past repeated actions.

Example Exercise:

Incorrect: I would have a big house when I was a child.
Correct: I used to have a big house when I was a child.
Solution:
The correct sentence uses "used to" to describe a state in the past, not a repeated action, which "would" would imply.

Misconception 5: Tenses Must Always Be Consistent Within a Sentence

While maintaining a consistent tense is generally a rule, there are instances where multiple tenses are used within the same sentence to accurately reflect the timing of actions. Narrative sentences often shift tenses to indicate a change in the time frame.

Example Exercise:

Incorrect: After she finishes her homework, she went to the gym.
Correct: After she finishes her homework, she will go to the gym.
Solution:
The correct sentence uses a present tense ("finishes") to refer to a future condition and a future tense ("will go") to describe the action that follows upon the completion of that condition.

To summarize, tenses are not always as straightforward as they seem. They are a nuanced aspect of English grammar that requires a deeper understanding of context, purpose, and convention to use correctly. Being aware of these common misconceptions can aid both English learners and native speakers in mastering the intricacies of tense usage. By practicing and applying these concepts, one can enhance their communication skills and avoid common errors.

Chapter 2: The Simple Present Tense

The simple present tense is a verb tense used to express actions that are habitual or generally true. This is a basic building block of English language grammar, which you will find in virtually any piece of writing or conversation.

Usage of the Simple Present Tense:

Routine or Habitual Actions: For actions that occur on a regular basis, such as daily tasks or routines. For example: "She walks to school every day."
General Truths: For facts that are always true. For instance: "The Earth revolves around the Sun."
Scheduled Events in the Near Future: Often for timetables or schedules. For example: "The train leaves at 6 PM tonight."
Instructions or Directions: It's commonly used in this context.
Headlines: Newspapers and summaries often use the simple present tense for immediate past actions. For example: "Company Shares Soar After Successful Launch."
Commentary: It's often used by commentators during live events. For instance: "The player shoots and he scores!"
The structure of the simple present tense is straightforward: it uses the base form of the verb for most subjects (I, you, we, they) and adds an 's' or 'es' for the third person singular (he, she, it).

Examples of verb conjugation in the simple present tense:

I/You/We/They walk.
He/She/It walks.
Negative sentences in the simple present tense typically use 'do not' or 'does not', followed by the base form of the verb.

I/You/We/They do not (don't) walk.
He/She/It does not (doesn't) walk.

Interrogative sentences in the simple present tense typically begin with 'do' or 'does', followed by the subject and the base form of the verb.

Do I/you/we/they walk?
Does he/she/it walk?
The simple present tense is technically rich because it can express a range of timeless concepts and habitual actions, and it is also versatile in terms of its practical applications, from giving instructions to describing laws of nature.

Rare Knowledge Content:
The simple present tense also carries a timeless aspect, often used in proverbs and maxims where the truth is not subject to time. Examples include sayings like "A stitch in time saves nine" or "History repeats itself." These sentences are not bound by the present moment but carry a truth that is considered universal and unchanging.

Practical Applications:

Coding and Programming: When writing comments or documentation in programming, the simple present is often used to describe functions or processes. Example: "This function calculates the total."
Cooking Recipes: Recipes use the simple present to give instructions. Example: "You mix the flour and sugar together."
Sports Commentary: To describe the action as it happens. Example: "He takes the shot and... he scores!"
Creative Style and Sample Exercises:

Let's dive into a few exercises that will help you practice the simple present tense.

Creating a Routine:

Write about your daily morning routine using the simple present tense.

Sample Answer: "Every morning, I wake up at 6 AM. I brush my teeth and make breakfast. Usually, I have eggs and toast. I read the newspaper as I eat. Then, I dress for work and leave my house by 7:30 AM."

Describing a Process:

Describe the process of photosynthesis using the simple present tense.

Sample Answer: Chlorophyll absorbs the sunlight, water, and carbon dioxide to produce glucose and oxygen. This process sustains the plant and releases oxygen into the atmosphere."

General Truths:

Write five sentences about general truths using the simple present tense.

Sample Answers: "Water boils at 100 degrees Celsius. The Earth orbits the Sun. Plants need sunlight to grow. Birds have feathers. Fish swim in water."

Giving Instructions:

Write a set of instructions for using an ATM.

Sample Answer: "First, insert your card into the machine. Then, enter your PIN when prompted. Select the 'Withdraw Cash' option. Choose the account type and enter the amount of cash you need. Finally, collect your cash and receipt."

By regularly practicing these exercises, you will become more comfortable with the simple present tense, understanding its nuances, and applying it correctly in various contexts.

When it comes to the English language, constructing sentences can be viewed as an art form. Whether affirmative, negative, or interrogative, each sentence structure has its own beauty and function within the fabric of communication.

Affirmative Sentences

Affirmative sentences state a fact or an opinion; they declare something is true or is in existence. They are the straight lines in the pattern of English, clear and direct. Typically, an affirmative sentence follows the Subject-Verb-Object (SVO) pattern.

For instance, consider the sentence, "The sun sets in the west." Here 'the sun' is the subject, 'sets' is the action or verb, and 'in the west' is the additional information or object complementing the verb. Affirmative sentences lay the foundation for stating truths and sharing information.

Sample Exercise: Creating Affirmative Sentences
Identify the subject (who or what is the sentence about?).
Determine the verb (what action is taking place?).
Add an object or complement (what additional information completes the thought?).
Exercise: Write an affirmative sentence using the following components:

Subject: A parrot
Verb: speaks
Object: words
Solution: "A parrot speaks words."

Negative Sentences

Negative sentences, on the other hand, are the dashes and dots, creating a pattern by denial or contradiction. They negate a statement or express that something is not true. The construction of a negative sentence in English often involves an auxiliary verb like 'do', 'be', or 'have', along with the adverb 'not'.

Take the sentence, "She does not like ice cream." The structure here is Subject-Auxiliary Verb-Negative-Verb-Object. The word 'not' follows the auxiliary verb 'does' to make the sentence negative.

Sample Exercise: Creating Negative Sentences
Begin with an affirmative sentence.
Introduce an auxiliary verb if one is not already present.
Place 'not' after the auxiliary verb.
Exercise: Convert the affirmative sentence "Cats climb trees." into a negative sentence.

Solution: "Cats do not climb trees."

Interrogative Sentences
Interrogative sentences are the question marks in the prose of English, inquiring and probing. They are designed to ask questions and require answers. The basic structure often involves inverting the order of the subject and the first auxiliary verb. If there is no auxiliary verb, 'do', 'does', or 'did' is typically used to initiate the question for present and past simple tenses.

Consider the question, "Is the train on time?"

Sample Exercise: Creating Interrogative Sentences
Identify the statement you want to inquire about.
Move the auxiliary verb before the subject.
If there's no auxiliary verb, use 'do/does/did' as appropriate.
Exercise: Formulate a question from the statement "He understands the lesson."

Solution: "Does he understand the lesson?"

Through these exercises, we see the importance of sentence structure in providing clarity and intent in communication. Each type of sentence serves a unique purpose, and mastering their formation is a critical component of language proficiency. The artful arrangement of words to form affirmative, negative, and interrogative sentences is not just a technical skill but a creative endeavor that can enhance our expression and understanding in daily communication.

Understanding the simple present tense is fundamental when learning or teaching English. It's a versatile tense that serves many functions, including the expression of habitual actions, general truths, and scheduled events.

Habitual Actions
Habitual actions are routines or activities that occur regularly. They can be daily, weekly, monthly, or any consistent pattern. When we describe these actions, we use the simple present tense. For example, "She walks to work every day." This sentence implies that the action of walking to work is a regular occurrence...

The simple present tense in English serves as a versatile tool, painting the canvas of everyday life with strokes of routine, inscribing the tablets of knowledge with immutable truths, and sketching out the blueprints of forthcoming endeavors. Here, we unfurl the narrative of Mark's quotidian existence, cast our gaze upon the unalterable verities of the botanical realm, and chart out the temporal map of scholarly pursuits and erudite congregations.

Crafting the Tapestry of Routine
Let us envision Mark, not merely as an office worker, but as the embodiment of discipline, with mornings orchestrated with the precision of a well-tuned symphony. His daybreak ritual unfurls as follows:

At the first whisper of 6 AM, Mark emerges from slumber's embrace.
With the morning freshness, he partakes in the ritual of purification and imbibes a chalice of verdant tea.
He joins the caravan of commuters aboard the 7:15 AM iron steed to the heart of the metropolis.
Upon the hour of eight, he embarks upon his daily odyssey of enterprise.
As the mechanical heart of his digital companion whirs to life, he delves into the realm of electronic missives.

Sample Exercise: Crafting a Morning Symphony in Simple Present

Craft sentences to depict your morning routine in the style of a symphonic movement using simple present tense.

Exercise Resolution:

As dawn breaks, I emerge from the world of dreams.
In the quietude of morning, I restore order to my resting sanctuary.
I break my fast with the robust simplicity of ovum and toasted grains.
I partake in the ritual of information, perusing the day's tidings.
At the appointed moment of 8:30 AM, I embark on my journey, entrusting my travels to the timely chariot of public transit.
Unveiling the Constants of Nature
Our exploration continues as we articulate the perennial truths of flora, not merely as static facts but as the enduring principles of life's green tapestry:

In their quiet majesty, plants bask in the golden radiance of the sun, thriving.
They quench their thirst from the earth's reservoirs with roots as conduits.
Through the alchemy of photosynthesis, they conjure sustenance from light.
The verdant foliage, with chlorophyll coursing through its veins, becomes the crucible of life.
As silent benefactors, plants bequeath the breath of oxygen to our shared atmosphere.
Sample Exercise: The Constants of Cyberspace

Devise sentences stating immutable truths about the digital realm of computers using simple present tense.

Exercise Resolution:

Within their silicon minds, computers orchestrate the flow of information with methodical precision.
They cradle our digital memories in the labyrinthine vaults of their storage.
We commune with these electronic entities through the talismans of input devices.
Through the incantations of software, we compel these machines to bend to our will and purpose.
Upon the foundation of an operating system, they marshal the legions of bytes and pixels in harmonious order.
The Chronograph of Planned Events
Lastly, we plot the temporal coordinates of a gathering of minds, not as a mere sequence of happenings but as the deliberate cadence of intellectual exchange:

With the punctuality of the rising sun, the conference awakens at 9 AM.
At the stroke of 10, the sage weaves wisdom into the keynote oration.
As the clock hands align at 11, a tapestry of breakout sessions unfolds.
The communal repast awaits in the dining sanctum as midday turns.
As daylight wanes, accolades are bestowed in a ceremonial tribute to excellence.
Sample Exercise: The School Day's Chronicle

Compose sentences outlining the day's scholarly chapters in a place of learning using simple present tense.

Exercise Resolution:

In the hallowed halls, the day's quest for knowledge commences at half-past the eighth hour.
Pupils venture into the sanctuary of the written word as the decagonal clock face marks the tenth hour.

The noonday bell heralds a convivial interlude for sustenance.

In the afternoon, the young adepts of science enter their laboratory domain as the hands of the clock point to two.

The day's scholastic journey reaches its denouement, and the steeds of travel depart at the half hour past three.

In these contexts, the simple present tense allows us to construct narratives that reflect the structured regularity of existence, the steadfast axioms of our universe, and the meticulous planning of human endeavors. It is a temporal chisel with which we carve out the everyday, the universal, and the scheduled in the language of the now.

Technical Aspects of Simple Present Tense

1. Verb Conjugation:
The base form of the verb is used with all personal pronouns except for third-person singular (he, she, it), where an -s or -es is added. For example, "talk" becomes "talks" with he, she, or it.

2. Negative Sentences:
We typically use the auxiliary "do not" or "does not" for negatives. For instance, "She does not like dancing."

3. Interrogative Sentences:
For questions, we invert the subject and the auxiliary verb "do" or "does". For example, "Does he play football?"

4. Non-Action Verbs:
Non-action verbs, or stative verbs, are not usually used in the simple present tense to talk about actions. They describe states, senses, desires, possession, etc.

5. Adverbs of Frequency:
Adverbs like "always", "usually", "often", "sometimes", "rarely", and "never" are used to indicate frequency and are usually placed before the main verb but after the verb "to be".

Rare Knowledge Content

Did you know that some languages do not use tense in the same way English does? For example, Mandarin Chinese does not conjugate verbs to indicate tense; the time of an action is understood from context or time-specific words. This is a fascinating aspect of cross-linguistic grammar studies, showing the uniqueness of English tense usage.

Practical Applications

Understanding the simple present tense is crucial for clear communication in English, whether in writing or speaking. It is essential for creating resumes, reports, or even in everyday conversation when discussing routines or schedules.

Creative Exercises

Exercise 1: Identifying Simple Present Tense

Read the paragraph and identify all the simple present tense verbs:

Birds chirp early in the morning. My neighbor walks his dog at 7 AM daily. The library closes at 8 PM."

Solution:

- Rises
- Sets
- Chirp
- Walks
- Closes

Exercise 2: Creating Sentences

Create five sentences using the simple present tense:

1. The dog _____ for food when it's hungry.

2. My brother _____ the guitar every evening.
3. The moon _____ around the Earth.
4. The bakery _____ the freshest bread.
5. She always _____ her homework on time.

Solution:

1. The dog barks for food when it's hungry.
2. My brother plays the guitar every evening.
3. The moon orbits around the Earth.
4. The bakery sells the freshest bread.
5. She always does her homework on time.

Exercise 3: Transforming Sentences

Transform the following sentences into negative and interrogative forms:

- "John works on the weekend."
- "Cats like milk."

Solution:

Negative:
- "John does not work on the weekend."
- "Cats do not like milk."

Interrogative:
- "Does John work on the weekend?"
- "Do cats like milk?"

By understanding and practicing the simple present tense, you can enhance your English communication greatly, giving you the ability to describe an array of everyday situations and facts accurately and effectively.

Chapter 3: The Present Continuous Tense

The present continuous tense is a form of the verb that shows something is happening now, at this moment, or is unfinished. It is often used to describe actions that are in progress at the time of speaking.

For instance, if you are eating a meal and speaking on the phone, you might say, "I am eating dinner." This sentence is in the present continuous tense. The structure of the present continuous tense is subject + am/is/are + verb-ing. The verb "to be" (am, is, are) changes depending on the subject (I, you, he, she, it, we, they).

Now, let's examine the usage of the present continuous tense in various situations:

Actions Happening Now: As mentioned, the present continuous tense is mainly used to express that an action is ongoing at the moment of speaking. For example, "She is reading a book." This means she started reading before now and is still reading at this moment.

Longer Actions in Progress: It's also used for a longer action in progress but not necessarily at the exact moment of speaking.

Planned Future Events: Surprisingly, we use this tense to talk about arranged future events. "They are meeting tomorrow." Even though it's a future event, the present continuous indicates a degree of certainty or a scheduled plan.

Annoying Habits: Interestingly, present continuous can also express annoyance at repeated actions, usually with "always," "constantly," or "continually." "He is always losing his keys." This isn't happening right now, but it's an ongoing situation that happens often.

Now, let's look at some rare knowledge about the present continuous tense:

It can express a change of situation or development: "Our company is growing quickly."

In some dialects of English, the present continuous can be used with the verb "go" to indicate a strong intention: "I am going to learn Italian."

Moving into the realm of technical content, let's understand some nuances:

Negatives: To make the present continuous negative, you add "not" after the verb "to be." "They are not coming to the party."

Questions: For questions, invert the subject and the verb "to be." "Is he reading the newspaper?"

Adverbs of Manner: These can often accompany the present continuous to describe the manner of the action. "She is speaking softly."

Let's translate this knowledge into some practical applications by crafting exercises.

Exercise 1: Construct five sentences using the present continuous tense to describe actions happening now.

Solutions:

"The children are playing in the park."
"I am typing an email to my colleague."
"He is cooking dinner for the family."
"We are discussing the project's timeline."

"The dog is barking at the mailman."
Exercise 2: Create negative sentences in the present continuous tense.

Solutions:

"They are not watching the movie anymore."
"I am not feeling very well right now."
"We are not making any noise."
Exercise 3: Formulate questions using the present continuous tense.

Solutions:

"Are you reading something interesting?"
"Is she working on the new project?"
"Are they coming to the meeting later?"
"Is it raining outside?"
"Are we meeting in the same conference room?"
By working through these exercises, you can see the present continuous tense in action and understand how it is used in various contexts. The key is to remember that it's not just for actions happening at the very moment but also for ongoing situations, planned future events, and even habitual actions that can be bothersome. By mastering the use of the present continuous tense, you can more precisely communicate a wide range of situations and actions in the English language.

Affirmative Sentences in the Present Continuous Tense
The Present Continuous Tense is employed when discussing actions currently in progress or plans that have been established for the near future. The structure typically follows a subject, the auxiliary verb "to be" in its correct form (am/is/are), followed by the verb with an -ing ending.

Let's explore how to construct an affirmative sentence in the Present Continuous Tense:

Subject + is/am/are + Verb(-ing)

Here are some examples:

I am writing a letter.
You are reading a book.
He is playing football.
She is dancing in the rain.
It is raining outside.
We are learning new skills.
They are working on a project.
In each of these sentences, the action is happening at the moment of speaking.

Sample Exercise: Forming Affirmative Sentences
Turn the following base sentences into affirmative Present Continuous sentences.

I (to eat) dinner.
She (to study) for her exams.
They (to build) a new house.
The dog (to bark) loudly.
The earth (to revolve) around the sun.
Solutions:
I am eating dinner.
She is studying for her exams.
They are building a new house.
The dog is barking loudly.
The earth is revolving around the sun.
Negative Sentences in the Present Continuous Tense
Negative sentences in the Present Continuous Tense are crafted by adding 'not' after the auxiliary verb 'to be'. This structure is essential when you want to express that an action is not occurring at the present moment.

Subject + is/am/are + not + Verb(-ing)

For instance:

I am not watching TV right now.
You are not listening to me.

He is not eating the cake.
She is not attending the meeting.
It is not working properly.
We are not going to the party.
They are not sleeping yet.
Each sentence communicates the absence of an action at the time of speaking.

Sample Exercise: Forming Negative Sentences
Make the following base sentences into negative Present Continuous sentences.

I (to play) the guitar.
You (to wear) your shoes.
The cat (to drink) milk.
Our team (to win) the match.
The sun (to set) right now.
Solutions:
I am not playing the guitar.
You are not wearing your shoes.
The cat is not drinking milk.
Our team is not winning the match.
The sun is not setting right now.
Interrogative Sentences in the Present Continuous Tense
Interrogative sentences in the Present Continuous Tense are formed to ask questions about actions in progress. The structure begins with the auxiliary 'to be', followed by the subject and the verb with an -ing ending.

Is/Am/Are + Subject + Verb(-ing)?

Consider the following examples:

Am I making sense?
Are you coming to the party?
Is he doing his homework?
Is she taking the train?
Is it snowing outside?
Are we meeting at eight?

Are they playing soccer?
Each question inquiries about an activity that may or may not be happening currently.

Sample Exercise: Forming Interrogative Sentences
Construct interrogative sentences from the following base sentences.

You (to enjoy) the concert.
The baby (to sleep) now.
The birds (to fly) south.
She (to consider) a new job.
The students (to prepare) for the exams.
Solutions:
Are you enjoying the concert?
Is the baby sleeping now?
Are the birds flying south?
Is she considering a new job?
Are the students preparing for the exams?
In conclusion, the Present Continuous Tense serves as a vital tool for expressing ongoing actions and immediate plans. The ability to form affirmative, negative, and interrogative sentences using this tense is fundamental in everyday communication. By practicing the construction of such sentences, one can enhance their mastery of the English language, allowing for clearer and more precise interactions.

The present continuous tense is a verb tense used to describe actions that are happening at the present moment, temporary situations, or to discuss future arrangements. It is formed using the present tense of the verb "to be" (am/is/are) followed by the present participle of the main verb (the -ing form). This tense is particularly versatile and offers a unique way to convey timing and intention in English.

Actions Happening at the Moment of Speaking
When we talk about actions happening right now, at the moment of speaking, we use the present continuous tense. This helps us convey the immediacy of the action.

Sample Exercise:

Imagine you are observing a cat chasing a mouse. Write a sentence describing this action using the present continuous tense.
Solution:

"The cat is chasing the mouse."
In this sentence, "is chasing" indicates that the action is happening at this very moment.

Temporary Situations
Temporary situations may not be happening at the exact moment of speaking but are occurring around the current period in time. The present continuous tense illustrates that the situation is temporary and likely to change in the future.

Sample Exercise:

Describe the work situation of a friend who has a short-term job.
Solution:

"She is working as a seasonal tour guide."
"Is working" in this context shows that her employment is temporary and expected to change when the season ends.

Future Arrangements
We also use the present continuous tense to discuss plans or arrangements that are scheduled or agreed upon for the future. This is a common and practical application of the tense, giving a sense of personal involvement in the plans.

Sample Exercise:

Write about your plans for a meeting with a friend next week using the present continuous tense.
Solution:

"I am meeting my friend next Wednesday for lunch."
Here, "am meeting" suggests a personal arrangement that has been set for the future.

The present continuous tense is not just a grammatical structure but a tool that brings language to life. It can express immediacy, a sense of temporary state, or planned actions. This tense helps to add precision and clarity, offering a window into when something is happening and what can be expected as either an ongoing process or in the imminent future.

Understanding and using the present continuous tense effectively can enhance both written and spoken communication. It is essential for conveying nuanced meanings and for accurately representing the timing of actions and events.

To continue with the practice:

Sample Exercise:

Compose a paragraph describing a situation where you are temporarily taking on different responsibilities than usual at work.
Solution:

"I am currently overseeing the client portfolio reviews, a task that typically falls outside my regular duties. As our team is transitioning between project managers, I am stepping in to ensure continuity. This week, I am also attending several networking events on behalf of our company. Additionally, I am collaborating with the marketing department to refine our outreach strategy. Though these responsibilities are not part of my normal job description, I am finding the challenges enriching and informative."
By practicing these exercises, one can gain proficiency in the present continuous tense, which is a fundamental part of

mastering English language tenses and enhancing one's communication skills.

The present continuous and the simple present tenses are two different ways to talk about actions and events in English.

The present continuous tense is used to describe actions that are happening at the moment of speaking or actions that are temporary. It is formed using the verb 'to be' (am/is/are) plus the '-ing' form of the main verb. For example, if I say, "I am reading a book," it means that I am in the middle of reading the book right now. It's a temporary action; I started reading before now, and I will finish reading at some point in the future.

In contrast, the simple present tense is used for routines, habits, and facts. It simply uses the base form of the verb for most subjects (I, you, we, they) and adds '-s' or '-es' for the third person singular (he, she, it). For instance, if I say, "She reads books every night," it implies that reading books is her regular habit, not something she is only doing right now.

Let's explore some rare knowledge and technical content regarding these tenses:

Aspect and Emphasis:
The present continuous tense is technically known as the "present progressive" because it describes ongoing action with a sense of progression. It has an active quality to it, emphasizing the process of the action. Meanwhile, the simple present often focuses on the general truth or habitual aspect of an action rather than its immediacy or progression.

Frequency Adverbs:
Adverbs of frequency such as "always," "usually," "sometimes," "rarely," and "never" are often used with the simple present to indicate routine or frequency. With the present continuous, you might use adverbs like "now," "right

now," "at the moment," or "currently" to stress the temporary or ongoing nature of an activity.

Non-Continuous Verbs:
Some verbs, especially those describing mental states, emotions, and senses, are typically not used in the continuous form. Verbs like "believe," "know," "love," "like," "hate," "want," "smell," "taste," and "hear" often do not take the continuous aspect, even when we are talking about the present moment. We would say, "I think it's a good idea," not "I am thinking it's a good idea," even if the thinking is happening right now.

Time Expressions:
Certain time expressions are often paired with these tenses. For instance, "today," "this week," "this year" are time frames that can be used with both tenses but would change the meaning slightly. Using them with the present continuous would suggest that the action is temporary within that time frame, whereas with the simple present, it would suggest a habit within the time frame.

Practical Applications:
Understanding the difference between these two tenses is crucial in everyday communication. When making arrangements or discussing plans, the present continuous is often more appropriate, as in "We are meeting at six." If you were to say, "We meet at six," it would suggest that meeting at six is what you regularly do, not a plan for one particular evening.

Now, let's put this knowledge into practice with some sample exercises.

Exercise 1:
Choose the correct tense for the following sentences (Present Continuous or Simple Present).

I _____ (to read) a fascinating book about history.

36

He _____ (to play) tennis on Saturdays.
The sun _____ (to shine) right now.
She usually _____ (to take) her dog for a walk in the evening.
They _____ (to plan) a holiday for next summer.
Solutions to Exercise 1:

I am reading (Present Continuous) a fascinating book about history. (The action is happening right now.)
He plays (Simple Present) tennis on Saturdays. (It indicates a habitual action.)
The sun is shining (Present Continuous) right now. (It describes an action happening at the moment.)
She usually takes (Simple Present) her dog for a walk in the evening. (It indicates a regular routine.)
They are planning (Present Continuous) a holiday for next summer. (It describes making future plans, which is currently in progress.)
Exercise 2:
Create sentences using the prompts, choosing the correct tense.

 (They / to eat / dinner / right now)
(You / to speak / English / fluently)
(It / to rain / often / in London)
(We / to work / on a project / this month)
Solutions to Exercise 2:

She watches TV every night. (Simple Present – it indicates a habit.)
They are eating dinner right now. (Present Continuous – it describes an action happening at the moment.)
You speak English fluently. (Simple Present – it indicates a general fact or state.)
It often rains in London. (Simple Present – it expresses a habitual action or general truth.)
We are working on a project this month. (Present Continuous – it describes a temporary action within a specified time frame.)

Grasping the nuances between the present continuous and simple present tenses enriches your communication skills, allowing for precise and clear expression of thoughts and actions.

Present continuous tense is a form of verb tense that is used to describe actions that are currently happening at the moment of speaking or actions that are ongoing. It can also refer to future plans or events that are already decided or arranged. Understanding and using the present continuous tense can enhance both your written and spoken English by allowing you to accurately convey actions in progress and future plans.

Technical Explanation:

In English grammar, the present continuous is formed with the present tense of the verb "to be" (am/is/are) followed by a present participle (the '-ing' form of the verb). For example: "I am eating," "She is running," "They are studying."

Creative Aspect:

Imagine a painter. Each brushstroke is a word, and the present continuous is like the motion of the brush on the canvas. The stroke begins, it moves, and it is still in motion – that's your action in the present continuous.

Practical Applications:

The practicality of present continuous tense is far-reaching. It's used in everyday conversations, such as telling a friend what you're doing right now ("I am reading a book"), in business settings to describe ongoing projects ("We are working on the annual report"), or in making plans ("They are meeting us at 6 PM").

Exercises:

Here are some exercises to help you practice the present continuous tense. Try to create sentences that reflect actions happening as you write or planned activities for the near future.

Use the present continuous tense to describe what someone in your family is doing right now.

Example:

Original Sentence: "My sister reads a book."
Present Continuous: "My sister is reading a book."
Create a sentence about a friend's plans for the evening using the present continuous tense.

Imagine you are in a park. Write five sentences describing what people are doing around you using the present continuous tense.

Sample Solution:

"Some children are playing soccer on the grass field."
"A group of musicians is setting up their instruments for a performance."
"Several dogs are chasing each other, their owners watching with amusement."
Write about the current state of a project you or someone you know is working on, using the present continuous tense.

Sample Solution:

"I am organizing the research data into comprehensive reports."
Describe your own routine on a typical morning using the present continuous tense.

Sample Solution:

"I am waking up to the sound of my alarm clock blaring."
"I am brushing my teeth while listening to the morning news."
"I am making coffee, the aroma filling the kitchen."
"I am choosing my clothes for the day, trying to decide what to wear."
By practicing these exercises, you can develop a stronger grasp of the present continuous tense, allowing you to describe ongoing actions and future arrangements with greater confidence. Remember, like any other skill, mastering a language structure requires patience and regular practice.

Chapter 4: The Present Perfect Tense

The present perfect tense is a fascinating aspect of English grammar that allows speakers to describe an action that has occurred in the past but is still relevant or influential in the present. This tense is unique because it bridges the past and the present, unlike the simple past tense, which is used for actions that were completed in the past and have no bearing on the present.

Usage of the present perfect tense involves a combination of the present tense form of the verb "to have" (either "have" or "has," depending on the subject) and the past participle of the main verb. For instance, "I have eaten," "She has gone," "We have seen." It's important to note that the past participle is not simply the past tense of a verb. In regular verbs, it is formed by adding -ed to the base form of the verb (e.g., "talk" becomes "talked"), but many verbs are irregular and have unique past participle forms (e.g., "eat" becomes "eaten").

The present perfect tense is used in several ways:

To describe an action that was completed at an unspecified time in the past. For example, "I have visited Paris." The exact time is not important or is not known.

To express life experiences.

To talk about changes over time.

For repeated actions that occurred at an undetermined time between the past and now. "He has read that book several times."

Let's delve into some sample exercises that illustrate the present perfect tense:

Exercise 1: Forming the Present Perfect Tense

Provide the present perfect form of the verb in parentheses.

They (to be) _____ friends for over a decade.
She (to write) _____ a letter to her pen pal.
I (to eat) _____ sushi before.
We (to see) _____ this movie several times.
He (never to travel) _____ abroad.
Answers:

They have been friends for over a decade.
She has written a letter to her pen pal.
I have eaten sushi before.
We have seen this movie several times.
He has never traveled abroad.
Exercise 2: Using the Present Perfect in Questions

Formulate questions in the present perfect tense using the prompts provided.

(you / to see) _____ the new exhibition?
(she / to complete) _____ her homework?
(they / to visit) _____ the new mall?
(he / to find) _____ his keys?
(we / to decide) _____ on the venue?
Answers:

Have you seen the new exhibition?
Has she completed her homework?
Have they visited the new mall?
Has he found his keys?
Have we decided on the venue?
Exercise 3: Negative Sentences in the Present Perfect

Create negative sentences in the present perfect using the following cues.

(I / not / to finish) _____ the report.
(she / not / to visit) _____ that country.

(they / not / to eat) _____ breakfast.
(he / not / to see) _____ that film.
(we / not / to understand) _____ the instructions.
Answers:

I have not finished the report.
She has not visited that country.
They have not eaten breakfast.
He has not seen that film.
We have not understood the instructions.
The present perfect tense is a bridge between past and present, and understanding it can greatly enhance your ability to express timing and relevance of events in English. It is a gateway to speaking about the past in a way that is vibrant and alive, ever touching the present moment. This tense is not just a grammatical rule; it is a narrative tool that allows speakers to connect times and experiences, adding depth to the language.

Affirmative Sentences in the Present Perfect Tense

The Present Perfect Tense represents an action that has been completed at some point in the past but is connected to the present, often when the exact time is not specified. It is formed using the auxiliary verb 'have' (or 'has' for third person singular subjects) followed by the past participle of the main verb.

In crafting affirmative sentences in the Present Perfect Tense, one must understand the structure, which typically follows the subject + have/has + past participle verb form. Here's an elaboration with varied sentence structures:

Simple affirmations often involve stating a completed action: "I have read the book." This straightforward sentence suggests that at some point recently, the speaker finished reading the book.

Adding details can enhance the sentence: "She has completed her masterpiece, which will soon be unveiled." This sentence not only conveys that the action is complete but also implies a future event related to the past action.

Describing an experience uses the same tense: "We have traveled to Iceland." It indicates that the act of traveling happened in the past, but the experience is relevant to the present.

Expressing changes over time: "He has grown so much since last year." This emphasizes the transformation that has occurred.

Listing multiple actions: "They have painted the fence, repaired the gate, and planted new flowers." Such a sentence communicates various completed actions related to a common theme or purpose.

Sample Exercise for Affirmative Sentences :

Write five affirmative sentences in the Present Perfect Tense about activities completed by someone today.

Solution:
She has finished her assignments.
He has started a new job.
They have made dinner for the family.
The gardener has watered all the plants.
The team has won its first match of the season.
Negative Sentences in the Present Perfect Tense

Negative sentences in the Present Perfect Tense convey that an action has not been completed at a certain time. This tense is formed with the subject + have/has + not + past participle verb form.

Denying completion: "I have not finished the report." This sentence indicates that the action of finishing the report is still pending.

Expressing the absence of experience: "We have not visited the new museum." Here, the sentence informs us that the experience of visiting the museum is still to be had.

Negating changes over time: "He has not changed much since we last met." The sentence reflects that there has been no noticeable change in the person since the last meeting.

Refuting multiple actions: "They have not learned to dance, sing, or play an instrument." It clearly lists a number of activities that have not been undertaken.

Rejecting the occurrence of an event: "The meeting has not taken place." This sentence denies that the meeting has occurred.

Sample Exercise for Negative Sentences:

Write five negative sentences in the Present Perfect Tense about activities that have not been done this week.

Solution:
She has not visited her grandmother this week.
The students have not submitted their essays.
We have not bought the tickets for the concert.
Our neighbors have not trimmed the hedge.
The committee has not selected a president.
Interrogative Sentences in the Present Perfect Tense

Interrogative sentences in the Present Perfect Tense are used to ask whether an action has been completed or not. They follow the structure: have/has + subject + past participle verb form?

Asking about completion: "Have you finished your meal?"

Probing changes over time: "Has he grown taller since last year?" This question investigates whether there has been a noticeable change in his height.

Questioning multiple actions: "Have they learned to cook, clean, or do laundry?"

Seeking confirmation of an event: "Has the package arrived?"

Sample Exercise for Interrogative Sentences:

Create five interrogative sentences in the Present Perfect Tense related to tasks one might need to complete around the house.

Solution:
Have you cleaned the kitchen?
Has the mail been sorted yet?
Have we replaced the broken lightbulbs?
Have the children done their homework?
In each type of sentence—affirmative, negative, and interrogative—understanding the structure and purpose of the Present Perfect Tense is essential. It captures the essence of actions related to the present moment in time, despite being completed in the past, and allows for a broad range of expression in English communication.

The present perfect tense is a fascinating aspect of the English language that allows speakers to relate past actions to the present in a seamless manner. This tense is formed by combining the auxiliary verb "have" or "has" with the past participle of a main verb. The resulting construction bridges the gap between past and present, making it particularly useful in various contexts.

Let's explore the three primary uses of the present perfect tense you've asked about: past actions with present relevance, experiences, and unfinished actions.

Past Actions with Present Relevance

The present perfect tense is often employed to discuss actions that occurred at an unspecified time in the past but continue to bear significance in the present. Unlike the simple past tense, which is used to talk about actions that happened at a specific time and are now concluded, the present perfect suggests that the action has some influence on the current situation.

Technical Explanation:

When using the present perfect for past actions with present relevance, we are often focusing on the result of the action rather than when it happened. This is a subtle but important distinction. For instance, if you were to say, "I have read the book," it suggests that the reading, which took place at some unspecified time in the past, is relevant now because you are now informed about the book's content.

Sample Exercise:

Write five sentences using the present perfect tense to express past actions with present relevance.

The engineers have developed a new prototype that will revolutionize the industry.
Scientists have discovered a new planet, which has characteristics similar to Earth.
She has completed the report, so we can now proceed with the project meeting.
The company has expanded its operations to include international markets.
The software has been updated to improve security measures.
Experiences
Another remarkable use of the present perfect tense is to discuss life experiences. This is particularly common when someone is talking about things they have done throughout

their life or during a certain period, but without specifying when.

Technical Explanation:

When we talk about experiences, we're often trying to convey what we have encountered or gone through without focusing on the specific time frames of those experiences. This use of the present perfect allows us to present a cumulative sense of our experiences. For example, "I have traveled to many countries" does not tell you when I traveled, but that over time I've accumulated travel experiences.

Sample Exercise:

Write five sentences using the present perfect tense to express experiences.

I have tried various cuisines from around the world.
She has written articles on a multitude of topics.
They have visited several remote islands during their travels.
We have participated in numerous community service projects.
He has learned to play several musical instruments.
Unfinished Actions
The present perfect tense is also exceptionally useful for indicating actions that started in the past and are still continuing now, or have been repeated up to the present.

Technical Explanation:

In this case, the present perfect tense gives us a sense of duration or continuity. Phrases like "have been" or "has been" often accompany time expressions such as "for," "since," and "all day." For example, "I have worked here for five years" indicates that you started working here five years ago and are still working here.

Sample Exercise:

Write five sentences using the present perfect tense to express unfinished actions.

She has been studying for the exam since Monday.
We have been experiencing some technical difficulties for the past hour.
He has been working on the new design all morning.
They have been living in this neighborhood for a decade.
The present perfect tense serves as a bridge between past events and the present moment, giving us a versatile tool for expressing a range of concepts from experience to continuity. It's an integral part of English that helps provide context, relevance, and connection to our everyday conversations and writing.

The English language has a wealth of tenses that express time in various ways. Two of these tenses, the present perfect and the simple past, are commonly used to talk about actions and events in relation to the present moment and the past. To explore these tenses thoroughly, let's embark on a detailed examination of each, their distinctions, and their uses.

Present Perfect Tense
The present perfect tense is a bit of a time-bender. It connects the past and the present in an intricate dance of time. This tense is not just about what happened; it's about the significance of past actions in the present moment.

Technical Content:
In a more technical light, the present perfect tense is characterized by its aspect, which linguists describe as "perfective." It signifies that an action or state has been completed at some point before now, yet it still has relevance or consequences in the present.

Practical Applications:
The present perfect is often used to talk about experiences, changes, or situations that have occurred over a period of time up to the present. For instance, if you say, "I have traveled to Japan," it implies that the experience of traveling to Japan happened at an undefined time in the past and is considered an important aspect of your life experiences as of now.

Creative Style with Sample Exercise:
Imagine time as a river flowing from the past towards you, standing in the present. The present perfect is like a net that catches various fish from any point upstream — but you are not saying exactly where or when you caught them, just that you have them now.

Exercise:

She _____ (write) three books.
I _____ (never/eat) sushi.
They _____ (live) in Berlin since 2010.
Solutions:

She has written three books.
I have never eaten sushi.
They have lived in Berlin since 2010.
Simple Past Tense
The simple past tense is straightforward: it deals purely with the past. This tense is formed by using the past form of the verb alone for regular verbs (ending in -ed) or the second form of the verb for irregular verbs. It's like pointing to a spot on the timeline and saying, "This happened right there, and nowhere else!"

Technical Content:
From a technical standpoint, the simple past is known as a "preterite" tense. It marks actions or situations that took place at a specific time and have no direct bearing on the

present moment. The focus is exclusively on the action or event itself, not on its continuation or effects.

Practical Applications:
You use the simple past when you want to mention when something happened or to describe a sequence of events in the past. If you say, "I traveled to Japan last year," you are specifying that the event took place at a particular time in the past and is over now.

Creative Style with Sample Exercise:
Think of the simple past as a photo album. Each picture is a complete scene from the past. You can point to a photo and say, "This is what I did." There is no direct link to the present, just a memory frozen in time.

Exercise:

She _____ (write) her first poem in 2008.
I _____ (eat) sushi last night.
They _____ (move) to Berlin in 2010.
Solutions:

She wrote her first poem in 2008.
I ate sushi last night.
They moved to Berlin in 2010.
Key Differences
The present perfect and the simple past may appear similar, but they serve different functions:

Timeline: The present perfect connects the past to the present, while the simple past stays within the bounds of the past.
Specificity of Time: The present perfect is less specific about the time of the action, whereas the simple past is more time-specific.
Consequence: Actions in the present perfect have some bearing on the present. In contrast, actions in the simple past do not.

Creative Metaphor for Distinction:
The present perfect is like a bridge between two time islands — the Past and the Present. The simple past, however, is a signpost on the island of the Past, marking a spot that was significant but isn't directly connected to where we are now.

By understanding these differences, you can more accurately express when and how certain events have occurred in your life, which is an invaluable skill in both spoken and written English.

Present Perfect Tense is a fascinating aspect of the English language, often used to link the past with the present. It is unique because it does not simply tell us what happened; it also suggests some connection with the present moment. The construction of the Present Perfect Tense involves the use of the auxiliary verb "have" (or "has" for third person singular) followed by the past participle of the main verb.

Let's begin with some technical knowledge before moving on to exercises and applications.

Technical Understanding:
The Present Perfect Tense serves several functions:

To Describe an Action that Occurred at an Unspecified Time in the Past:
Here, the exact time is not important or not known. For example: "She has visited the Eiffel Tower."

To Talk About Life Experiences:
It is often used when discussing experiences up to now. For example: "I have tried sushi."

To Describe an Action That Started in the Past and is Still Continuing:
Words like "since" and "for" often appear in these sentences.

For Actions Repeated in an Unspecified Period Between the Past and Now:
For example: "We have watched that movie several times."

For Something That Was Done Recently, Often With Results in the Present:
For example: "I have just finished my homework."

The form "has/have + past participle" is consistent regardless of the subject. The past participle for regular verbs is the same as the past simple form, often ending in "-ed." For irregular verbs, the past participle varies and must be learned separately (e.g., "eaten," "flown," "gone").

Sample Exercises:
Exercise 1: Completion
Fill in the blanks with the correct form of the verb in parentheses to form the present perfect tense.

She _____ (write) three books this year.
I _____ (never/see) such a beautiful painting.
They _____ (live) in this city since 2010.
It _____ (just/start) to rain.
John _____ (be) to the new museum twice this month.
Solutions to Exercise 1:

She has written three books this year.
I have never seen such a beautiful painting.
They have lived in this city since 2010.
It has just started to rain.
John has been to the new museum twice this month.
Exercise 2: True or False?
Decide if the sentences use the present perfect tense correctly. If the sentence is false, correct it.

We has seen that movie last night.
She has been a teacher for twenty years.
They have ate sushi before.
I have learned three new languages.

He have just finished his meal.
Solutions to Exercise 2:

False (We have seen that movie last night.) - Correction: The present perfect is not typically used with a specific time like "last night." A better sentence might be, "We have seen that movie."
True
False (They have ate sushi before.) - Correction: "They have eaten sushi before."
True
False (He have just finished his meal.) - Correction: "He has just finished his meal."
Exercise 3: Rewrite Sentences
Rewrite the following sentences in the present perfect tense.

She finishes her assignment.
They play football every Saturday.
John eats the whole cake.
We visit our grandmother in June.
The children do their chores.
Solutions to Exercise 3:

She has finished her assignment.
They have played football many Saturdays.
John has eaten the whole cake.
We have visited our grandmother in June. (Note: The use of "in June" suggests a specific time, which is generally not used with present perfect. However, if June is not yet over, or if we are referring to multiple Junes in the past, it could be correct.)
The children have done their chores.
Practical Applications:
The Present Perfect Tense isn't just a grammatical exercise; it has real-life applications that can enhance your communication skills, especially in formal settings. For instance:

In Professional Environments:

When you're updating your resume or discussing your work experience in an interview, you'll often use the present perfect to describe your responsibilities and accomplishments.

In Academic Settings:
When writing about historical events or literature in essays, the present perfect can be used to connect past events or actions to the present-day discussion.

In Everyday Conversations:
When catching up with friends or telling stories, the present perfect is a way to share experiences or talk about changes. For example: "She has grown so much since I last saw her."

Understanding and using the present perfect can connect you more deeply to English speakers and their culture. It is a gateway to not just telling others about your life, but also engaging with theirs, as it prompts people to reflect on their experiences and share their stories up until now.

In conclusion, the Present Perfect Tense is a versatile and essential component of English that helps to convey a deep sense of time and experience. By practicing the exercises and recognizing its practical applications, you can enhance your command of English in both personal and professional contexts.

Chapter 5: The Simple Past Tense

The simple past tense is a verb tense that is used to describe actions that were completed at a specific point in time in the past. It is among the most commonly used tenses in English, and mastering it is crucial for effective communication. The structure of the simple past tense is straightforward: for regular verbs, you add "-ed" to the base form of the verb to create the past tense. For instance, "walk" becomes "walked," and "listen" becomes "listened." However, there are many irregular verbs that do not follow this pattern, such as "go," which becomes "went," or "be," which turns into "was" or "were" depending on the subject.

In writing and speaking, we utilize the simple past tense for several key reasons. Firstly, it allows us to tell stories and recount events that have already happened. When sharing our experiences, such as what we did on our last vacation, we rely on the simple past tense: "I visited the museum," or "We ate at a new restaurant." It also lets us report past facts or generalizations, as in "Shakespeare wrote many plays" or "Dinosaurs roamed the earth millions of years ago."

In technical contexts, the simple past is frequently employed to describe the methodology of experiments or procedures that were performed, for example, "The scientists conducted the experiment under controlled conditions." This use underscores the completion of an action, which is essential to distinguish between ongoing research and completed studies.

Understanding the simple past tense also involves recognizing its irregular forms, which can often be a challenge due to their lack of a consistent pattern. To become proficient, it is useful to study and memorize these forms, as they are commonly used in both spoken and written English.

Now, let's engage our creative side with some unique content focusing on the practical applications of the simple past tense.

Imagine a world where the fabric of history is woven by the threads of stories told in the simple past tense. Every monument we visit, every old book we leaf through, every aged photograph we peer at captures a narrative crystallized in this tense. History comes alive in sentences like "The Wright brothers flew the first powered aircraft in 1903," or "Neil Armstrong walked on the moon in 1969."

In the realm of literature, the simple past is the skeletal structure of storytelling. It paints pictures of bygone eras and allows characters to walk through time. Think of a classic like Charles Dickens' "A Tale of Two Cities," where the famous opening line "It was the best of times, it was the worst of times..." instantly plunges the reader into the past.

Additionally, in everyday practical applications, the simple past serves as a linguistic bridge connecting different generations. Grandparents recount tales to their grandchildren, beginning with phrases like "When I was your age..." enabling a shared connection through the recollection of past experiences.

Let's move on to a more technical aspect. In the field of research, the simple past tense is the gatekeeper of empirical data and findings. Scholars writing research papers or presenting findings use this tense to offer a chronological sequence of their research actions: "We tested the hypothesis," "We analyzed the data,"

To deepen our understanding, let's devise some sample exercises that utilize the simple past tense.

Exercise 1: Create five sentences using the simple past tense to describe actions completed yesterday.

I finished reading a novel yesterday.
She baked a chocolate cake for the party.
They played football in the park despite the rain.
The cat knocked over the vase when we were not home.
We discovered a new cafe and tried their specialty coffee.
Exercise 2: Convert the following sentences from the present tense to the simple past tense.

I walk to the store. (I walked to the store.)
She sings beautifully. (She sang beautifully.)
They go to the cinema every Friday. (They went to the cinema last Friday.)
The sun sets at eight o'clock. (The sun set at eight o'clock.)
He drives to work every day. (He drove to work yesterday.)
Exercise 3: Write a short paragraph about a historical event using the simple past tense.

In 1969, the world watched in awe as Apollo 11 completed its mission to the moon. Astronauts Neil Armstrong and Edwin "Buzz" Aldrin landed the lunar module, Eagle, on the moon's surface. Armstrong took the first steps on the moon, declaring, "That's one small step for man, one giant leap for mankind." They collected moon rocks and conducted experiments before returning safely to Earth. This monumental event changed space exploration forever.

In conclusion, the simple past tense is not just a grammatical form but a key to unlocking stories of the past, making sense of historical events, and sharing personal experiences. Its value is immense across various fields, from literature and history to technical research and daily communication. It enables us to paint vivid pictures of moments gone by and to relay completed actions with clarity and precision.

Understanding the simple past tense in English involves recognizing how it is used to express actions that have been completed at a specific time in the past. The formation of affirmative, negative, and interrogative sentences in the simple past tense is foundational to mastering past events' narration. Let's delve into each of these sentence types, accompanied by creative examples and exercises to help solidify the concepts.

Affirmative Sentences in Simple Past Tense

Affirmative sentences in the simple past tense state that an action or event occurred or a situation existed in the past. The structure is straightforward: you take the subject (I, you, we, they, he, she, it) and follow it with the verb in the past tense. For most regular verbs, this involves adding '-ed' to the base form. However, English is peppered with irregular verbs that defy this rule and must be learned individually.

Example:

I walked to the park.
She thought about the question.
They danced all night.
Technical Content:
To form an affirmative sentence in the simple past tense, you need to know the past tense form of the verb. With regular verbs, you can typically add "-ed" to the verb's base form. If the verb ends in 'e', like 'dance', you simply add 'd' to make 'danced'. With irregular verbs, there is no single rule; these verbs have unique past tense forms that must be memorized, like 'go' becomes 'went' and 'buy' becomes 'bought'.

Rare Knowledge:
The origins of many irregular verbs in English can be traced back to Old English, where strong verbs would change their vowel sounds to indicate tense, a process known as ablaut. Some of these old forms have survived into modern English as irregular verbs.

Sample Exercise:

Convert the following sentences to affirmative simple past tense:
I (to walk) to the market.

She (to read) a book.
They (to have) a party last night.
Solution:

I walked to the market.
She read a book.
They had a party last night.
Negative Sentences in Simple Past Tense
To form a negative sentence in the simple past tense, you combine the subject with 'did not' (or the contraction 'didn't') followed by the base form of the verb, regardless of whether it is regular or irregular.

Example:

I did not walk to the park.
She did not think about the question.
They did not dance all night.
Technical Content:
The 'did not' serves as an auxiliary or helper verb and is crucial in forming negatives in the simple past tense. The main verb reverts to its base form because the auxiliary 'did' already imply the past tense.

Rare Knowledge:
In Old English, negation could sometimes be achieved by simply adding 'ne' before the verb. Modern English has abandoned this simplicity for a more complex auxiliary system.

Sample Exercise:

Convert the following sentences to negative simple past tense:
I (to walk) to the market.
She (to read) a book.
They (to have) a party last night.

Solution:

I did not walk to the market.
She did not read a book.
They did not have a party last night.
Interrogative Sentences in Simple Past Tense
Interrogative sentences in the simple past are used to ask about actions or situations in the past. They typically begin with 'Did', followed by the subject and the base form of the verb.

Example:

Did you walk to the park?
Did she think about the question?
Did they dance all night?
Technical Content:
The interrogative form in the simple past tense requires inversion between the subject and the auxiliary verb 'did'. The main verb remains in its base form. This inversion is a common feature in English questions.

Rare Knowledge:
The auxiliary 'did' is actually the past tense of 'do', which in Middle English was used to give emphasis in statements. Its use in questions is a linguistic evolution that facilitated clearer communication.

Sample Exercise:

Convert the following sentences to interrogative simple past tense:
You (to walk) to the market.
She (to read) a book.
They (to have) a party last night.
Solution:

Did you walk to the market?
Did she read a book?

Did they have a party last night?
Each of these exercises highlights the practical application of past tense forms in everyday communication. By practicing the formation of affirmative, negative, and interrogative sentences, one can gain proficiency in recounting past experiences and events with clarity and precision. Understanding these structures also provides a stepping stone towards mastering more complex aspects of the English language, such as mixed tenses and conditional sentences.

The simple past tense in English is a verb tense that is used to describe actions, habits, and states that were completed at a specific time in the past. This form is one of the most commonly used tenses in English and is vital for talking about history, sharing experiences, and telling stories. It is recognized by its regular ending -ed for regular verbs, but it also has many irregular verbs with various past forms.

Completed Actions in the Past

When we talk about actions that happened and finished in the past, we use the simple past tense. It is not important when the action happened; what is important is that it is not happening now. For instance, if I say, "I watched a movie last night," it means that last night I started and finished watching a movie. The action is complete and belongs to the past.

Sample Exercise: Completed Actions in the Past

Create a sentence about a completed action from yesterday. Write a short narrative about an event that happened in the past year.
Solutions

"I visited the botanical garden yesterday."

"Last year, during a brisk autumn morning, I embarked on a journey to climb the Blue Mountain Peak. The climb was arduous and took the better part of the day. When I reached the summit, the view of the sun rising above the clouds was breathtaking. After spending an hour on the peak, I descended back to the base, where a sense of accomplishment filled my heart."

Past Habits

The simple past is also used to talk about habits in the past, actions that were done regularly or repeatedly. To describe such past habits, we often use time expressions like "when I was a child," "every day," or "on Sundays." For example, "When I was a child, I played outside every day." This tells us that playing outside was a regular activity in the past for me as a child.

Sample Exercise: Past Habits

Think of a hobby you used to do regularly but no longer practice. Write about it.
Describe a family tradition from your childhood.
Solutions

"In my teenage years, I used to collect stamps from different countries. Every weekend, I spent hours examining the intricate designs and learning about the cultures they represented. This hobby brought a sense of global connection to my small bedroom, but as I grew older, other interests took precedence, and my stamp collection was tucked away into the attic."

"Growing up, our family had a Sunday tradition of dining at our grandmother's house. The aroma of her famous roast chicken would greet us as we walked through the door. After dinner, we often gathered around the piano, singing old songs while our uncle played the tunes. These moments etched a sense of harmony and joy in my memory, recurring every week without fail."

Past States

We also use the simple past to describe states in the past which are no longer true. For example, "I was a student." This indicates that I am no longer a student now, but I was in the past.

Sample Exercise: Past States

Describe a state of mind or a feeling you had during a past event.
Recall a past job or role you had and describe it.
Solutions

"During the final match of the high school football championship, I was nervous. My hands were clammy, and my heart raced as I stood on the field. The weight of expectation lay heavily on my shoulders, and the roar of the crowd was both intimidating and exhilarating."
My days were spent among towering shelves of books, assisting patrons with research, and organizing community reading events. The role was one of quiet dedication to the spread of knowledge and the nurturing of a love for reading."
Understanding and using the simple past tense effectively allows for clear communication about the past, and these exercises should help solidify comprehension of its various uses. Engaging with the past tense in creative and reflective writing can open up avenues for sharing experiences and telling stories that resonate with others, each narrative a glimpse into a moment that, once present, has transformed into history.

The simple past tense in English is a verb tense that is used to describe actions that were completed in the past. It is a fundamental aspect of English grammar, essential for clear communication regarding past events. To delve into this area, one must understand the distinction between regular and irregular verbs.

Regular Verbs
Regular verbs are words that conform to a standard pattern when transitioning from their base form into the past tense. This transformation typically involves the addition of "-ed" to the end of the infinitive (the base form of the verb). For instance, the verb "walk" becomes "walked," and "jump" becomes "jumped."

The application of regular verbs is quite straightforward due to their predictable nature. Regardless of the subject, the verb remains unchanged, and the only modification is the addition of the past tense ending. This consistency allows learners to apply a simple rule across a broad spectrum of verbs.

Example Exercise for Regular Verbs:

Transform the following regular verbs to their past tense forms:
play
wash
guess
try
stop
Solution:

Played
Washed
Guessed
Tried (noting the y to i change before adding -ed)
Stopped (noting the doubling of the 'p' before adding -ed)
Irregular Verbs
On the other side of the spectrum are irregular verbs. These verbs do not follow a set pattern when changing into the past tense. The alteration can be unpredictable and must often be learned individually. For example, "go" becomes "went," and "eat" becomes "ate." There are no clear rules that govern these transformations, which makes them more challenging to master.

Irregular verbs can be tricky because they do not conform to a single formula. Their forms must be memorized, and it's often through practice and repeated exposure that one becomes familiar with them.

Example Exercise for Irregular Verbs:

Convert the following irregular verbs to their simple past tense forms:
bring
begin
go
see
have
Solution:

Brought
Began
Went
Saw
Had
Practical Applications
The practical applications of understanding the simple past tense with both regular and irregular verbs are immense. When writing a resume, for example, you often need to describe previous job responsibilities or accomplishments, which requires the simple past tense. Similarly, recounting personal experiences, narrating stories, or reporting historical facts also necessitate the use of the simple past.

Consider a historian drafting a report. To describe events that occurred, they would need to apply the simple past tense. For example: "Leonardo da Vinci painted the Mona Lisa in the 16th century." The verb "painted" is a regular verb that follows the standard -ed pattern.

In another case, imagine a traveler recounting their journey: "I went to the market, and then I saw a parade." The words "went" and "saw" are both irregular verbs that change form entirely in the past tense.

Rare Knowledge Content
It is fascinating to explore the origins of some irregular verbs, which often lie in the history of the English language itself. Many irregular verbs are holdovers from Old English, where different patterns of conjugation were more common. Over time, as the language evolved, most verbs regularized, but some, especially those that are used frequently, retained their irregular forms. This historical holdover is why we have such a diversity of verb forms today.

Technical Knowledge Content
Linguists classify verbs into groups known as "conjugation classes" or "morphological classes." Regular verbs fall into a class that applies the same morphological rule (adding -ed), while irregular verbs belong to several classes with various rules. Understanding these classes can deepen one's appreciation for the complexity of language development.

Creative Style Writing Exercise
Imagine a world where irregular verbs did not exist, and every verb followed the same pattern. Write a short paragraph about a day in the past, using only what would be regular verbs in this imagined world.

Sample Paragraph:

Yesterday, I waked up with the sunrise. I eated a hearty breakfast of eggs and toasts. I readed my favorite book for an hour, then I goed to the park. In the afternoon, I finded a quaint cafe and writed in my journal. It was a peaceful day, and I enjoyed every moment.

Exercise Solution:

Yesterday, I woke up with the sunrise. I ate a hearty breakfast of eggs and toast. I read my favorite book for an hour, then I went to the park. In the afternoon, I found a quaint cafe and wrote in my journal. It was a peaceful day, and I enjoyed every moment.

The exercise demonstrates the complexity and beauty irregular verbs add to the English language. Without them, the language might be simpler, but it would lose a part of its richness and history. The irregular verbs make English unpredictable at times, but also vivid and dynamic.

It is formed by using the past form of the verb, which often ends in -ed for regular verbs but can vary for irregular verbs. Let's delve into understanding, practicing, and mastering the simple past tense with a unique perspective, combining rare knowledge and practical application.

Understanding Simple Past Tense
To begin, the simple past tense is a verb tense that is used to talk about things that happened or existed before now. Imagine you are looking back at the past, and you want to describe events that have finished, such as historical events, personal experiences, or completed actions. This is where the simple past tense comes into play.

Technical Knowledge:
In technical terms, the simple past tense is used to express four main types of actions:

Completed Actions: Actions that started and finished at a specific time in the past.
A Series of Completed Actions: Several actions that occurred in the past one after another.
Habitual Actions in the Past: Actions that were done regularly in the past but not anymore.
Past Facts or Generalizations: Statements about the past that were generally true but not necessarily anymore.
Regular Verbs
Regular verbs in the simple past tense are easy to form because they follow a pattern.

Sample Exercise:
Write the simple past tense form of the following verbs:

Jump
Listen
Call
Paint
Ask
Solutions:

Jumped
Listened
Called
Painted
Asked
Irregular Verbs
Irregular verbs do not follow the regular pattern and can have different endings or completely change in the past tense. For example, 'go' becomes 'went', and 'see' becomes 'saw'.

Sample Exercise:

Run
Begin
Drink
Sing
Grow
Solutions:

Ran
Began
Drank
Sang
Grew
Rare Knowledge Content: Historical Linguistics
From a historical linguistics perspective, the simple past tense in English is a relic from a deeper past. It evolved from a system that used to include a present tense, a past tense,

and a perfect tense. Over time, English simplified to the two-tense system we have now, leaving us with the simple past as a way to denote actions that are completed.

Practical Application
Understanding the past tense is crucial in many fields, such as history, where accurate descriptions of past events are essential. It is also important in everyday communication when sharing experiences or telling stories.

Sample Exercise: Historical Reporting
Write a brief historical report using the simple past tense:

The Wright brothers _____ (1. invent) the first successful airplane. On December 17, 1903, they _____ (2. conduct) their first flight. Wilbur _____ (3. pilot) the plane for 59 seconds. Afterward, they _____ (4. continue) to improve their designs. Their achievements _____ (5. change) transportation forever.

Solutions:

The Wright brothers invented the first successful airplane. On December 17, 1903, they conducted their first flight. Wilbur piloted the plane for 59 seconds. Afterward, they continued to improve their designs. Their achievements changed transportation forever.

More Creative Style: A Short Story
To end our journey with the simple past tense, let's get creative. Here's a short story exercise for you to practice:

Sample Exercise: Short Story Completion
Complete the short story using the simple past tense:

Long ago, there _____ (1. be) a mysterious forest. Inside the forest, there _____ (2. live) creatures of old lore. One day, a brave explorer _____ (3. enter) the woods. She _____ (4. carry) a notebook, a compass, and an insatiable curiosity. She _____ (5. hope) to discover something unknown.

Solutions:

Long ago, there was a mysterious forest. Inside the forest, there lived creatures of old lore. One day, a brave explorer entered the woods. She carried a notebook, a compass, and an insatiable curiosity. She hoped to discover something unknown.

By exploring the technicalities of the simple past tense through exercises and creative storytelling, you can strengthen your grasp of past actions and their implications in both historical and modern contexts. Whether you're recounting the past or weaving a tale, the simple past tense is your gateway to narratives anchored in times gone by.

Chapter 6: The Past Continuous Tense

Definition of the Past Continuous Tense
The past continuous tense, also known as the past progressive tense, is a verb tense used to describe actions that were ongoing at a specific moment in the past. This tense provides a backdrop to events that were happening when something else occurred or to indicate that an action was in progress over a period of time in the past. The structure of the past continuous tense is straightforward: it combines the past tense of the verb 'to be' (was/were) with the present participle of the main verb (the -ing form).

Usage of the Past Continuous Tense
The usage of the past continuous is quite versatile. It's commonly used in the following situations:

To describe an action that was in progress at a specific time in the past: Here, the focus is on the process of the action rather than its completion.
To indicate that a longer action in the past was interrupted: The interruption is usually expressed with the past simple tense.
To describe two or more actions that were happening at the same time: These actions are usually parallel and ongoing.
To describe the atmosphere, setting, or background of a past event: It sets the scene for a narrative about past events.
To indicate a habitual action in the past: Especially when expressing irritation or amusement about that habit.
Unique and Rare Knowledge About the Past Continuous Tense
The past continuous tense can also be employed in a literary context to enhance the vividness of a narrative. It allows the writer to slow down the action, giving the reader a chance to immerse themselves in the ongoing scene. It can create a sense of development and suspense in a story.

Another less commonly discussed application of the past continuous tense is in reported speech. When reporting what

72

someone was saying or thinking at a particular moment in the past, the past continuous can be used to retain the continuous aspect of the original speech or thought.

Technical Content Related to the Past Continuous Tense
From a linguistic point of view, the past continuous tense is an aspect of the verb that shows the action's time-relative to the speaker's perspective. It employs auxiliary verbs and participles, which belong to the category of verb morphology known as aspect. Aspects in English grammar convey how an action extends over time, and the continuous aspect indicates that an action was ongoing.

In English, there are rules governing the co-occurrence of verb tenses known as "sequence of tenses," which sometimes require the use of the past continuous to maintain grammatical cohesion within a sentence or paragraph.

Practical Applications of the Past Continuous Tense
In practical terms, the past continuous can be used to:

Create engaging stories by setting scenes.
Describe past routines in personal biographies.
Share detailed eyewitness accounts where timing and sequence are important.
Offer explanations of events or behaviors that unfolded over a period of time.
Provide rich descriptions in historical accounts.
Sample Exercises and Solutions
Exercise 1: Create sentences using the past continuous tense to describe what each person was doing at 3 PM yesterday.

John (to work) on his new painting.
Susan and Michael (to walk) their dogs in the park.
The children (to play) in the backyard.
Mr. Thompson (to teach) his class about the past continuous tense.

Solutions:

John was working on his new painting.
Susan and Michael were walking their dogs in the park.
The children were playing in the backyard.
Mr. Thompson was teaching his class about the past continuous tense.
Exercise 2: Combine the following pairs of sentences into one using the past continuous and past simple tenses.

The phone rang. I was taking a shower.
She found her keys. She was looking under the couch.
The sun set. They were still hiking.
I heard a scream. I was walking through the forest.
Solutions:

She found her keys while she was looking under the couch.
They were still hiking when the sun set.
I was walking through the forest when I heard a scream.
The past continuous tense is not merely a grammatical structure; it is a tool that, when wielded with skill, can paint pictures of past events as if they are unfolding before our eyes. It allows language to breathe life into memories, making the bygone moments pulse with the immediacy of the present.

To convey this tense in English, we use the auxiliary verb "was" or "were" with the -ing form of the main verb.

Affirmative Sentences in Past Continuous Tense
An affirmative sentence in the past continuous tense states that an action was occurring at a certain time. The structure is straightforward: the subject is followed by "was" (for I, he, she, it) or "were" (for you, we, they), and then the base verb with an -ing ending.

Structure:

Subject + was/were + verb(-ing) + (object) + time reference

Example:

The birds were singing melodiously at dawn.
Technical Insight:
Here, "the birds" is the subject, "were" is the auxiliary verb, "singing" is the present participle form of "sing," and "at dawn" is the time reference indicating when the action was happening.

Sample Exercise:
Create five affirmative past continuous sentences using the verbs: walk, study, rain, cook, and dance.

Susan was walking through the park when the sun began to set.
Thomas and his classmates were studying diligently for the chemistry exam last night.
It was raining steadily throughout the early morning hours.
The chef was cooking an exquisite French dish when I arrived.
The couple was dancing gracefully under the starlit sky.
Negative Sentences in Past Continuous Tense
Negative sentences express that an action was not happening at a certain time in the past. To construct a negative sentence, we insert "not" between the auxiliary verb and the main verb.

Structure:

Subject + was/were + not + verb(-ing) + (object) + time reference
Example:

I was not feeling well yesterday evening.
Technical Insight:
In the above example, "I" is the subject, "was not" is the negated auxiliary verb, "feeling" is the present participle form of "feel," and "yesterday evening" specifies the time.

Sample Exercise:
Form five negative past continuous sentences using the verbs given in the affirmative exercise.

Susan was not walking through the park when it began to snow heavily.
Thomas and his classmates were not studying when the power went out.
It was not raining when I decided to leave the house.
The chef was not cooking when the kitchen timer went off.
The couple was not dancing when the music suddenly stopped.

Interrogative Sentences in Past Continuous Tense
Interrogative sentences ask if an action was occurring at a certain time in the past. They are formed by beginning the sentence with "was" or "were," followed by the subject and the present participle form of the verb.

Structure:

Was/Were + subject + verb(-ing) + (object) + time reference?
Example:

Were the children sleeping when the clock struck midnight?
Technical Insight:
In this question, "Were" is the auxiliary verb used for the plural subject "the children," "sleeping" is the present participle of "sleep," and "when the clock struck midnight" sets the time context.

Sample Exercise:
Construct five interrogative sentences based on the verbs used previously.

Was Susan walking through the park when the festival started?
Were Thomas and his classmates studying when the bell rang?

Was it raining when the parade was scheduled to begin?
Was the chef cooking the main course when the guests arrived?
Were the couple dancing when the announcement was made?
Solving the Exercise:
Now, let's answer these questions as if we were witnesses to these scenarios.

Yes, Susan was walking through the park when the festival started.
No, Thomas and his classmates were not studying; they were taking a break when the bell rang.
No, it was not raining; the weather was clear when the parade was scheduled to begin.
Yes, the chef was cooking the main course when the guests arrived.
Yes, the couple was dancing when the announcement was made.
By understanding the structure and the technique to form affirmative, negative, and interrogative sentences in the past continuous tense, one can articulate the nuances of past actions with clarity. Remember, the past continuous tense not only communicates the action but also paints a picture of the continuous nature of the action during a specific past time frame. This can add depth to storytelling, descriptions, and recollections of past events.

Understanding Past Continuous Tense
Past Continuous Tense is a verb form that indicates that an action was ongoing at a certain point in time in the past. It is formed using the past tense of the verb 'to be' (was/were) followed by the present participle (verb+ing).

Actions in Progress at a Specific Time in the Past
When you want to talk about an action that was happening at a particular moment in the past, the past continuous tense comes into play. It's like painting a picture where the action

hasn't finished, it's in the middle, ongoing, and the canvas is the specific time you're talking about.

For example, imagine a painting depicting a scene from yesterday at five o'clock. If someone was reading a book at that precise moment, you would say, "At five o'clock, she was reading a book." The action (reading) was in full swing and had not yet finished.

Interrupted Actions
In storytelling, we often discuss one action that is cut off by another. The past continuous sets the stage for that initial action, while the simple past interrupts it. Think of it as a music track that is smoothly playing in the background (past continuous) until a sound (simple past) abruptly stops it.

Consider this scenario: "She was walking her dog when the phone rang." Here, 'walking her dog' is the background track that was interrupted by the ringing phone.

Background Information
The past continuous also acts as a backdrop to a story by providing context or background information. It's like the setting of a stage before the main actors come on. This use gives readers a sense of atmosphere and a deeper understanding of the main events.

An example is, "The band was playing loud music as the guests arrived." The ongoing music sets the scene for the guests' arrival.

Sample Exercises with Solutions
Now, let's engage with some exercises to apply our understanding practically.

Exercise 1: Completing Sentences with Past Continuous Tense
Fill in the blanks with the correct form of past continuous tense of the verbs in parentheses.

I _____ (watch) a movie when he called.
They _____ (drive) to work when it started raining.
The children _____ (play) in the park at 4 PM yesterday.
She _____ (cook) dinner when the power went out.
We _____ (discuss) the project, when suddenly the alarm _____ (ring).
Solutions

I was watching a movie when he called.
They were driving to work when it started raining.
The children were playing in the park at 4 PM yesterday.
We were discussing the project, when suddenly the alarm rang.
Exercise 2: Identifying Uses of Past Continuous Tense
Identify what the past continuous tense is depicting in the following sentences: action in progress, interrupted action, or background information.

The sun was setting as the ceremony began.
They were having dinner when the guests arrived.
I was studying for my exams all night.
It was raining throughout the night.
Solutions

Background Information - The sunset provides the setting for the ceremony's beginning.
Interrupted Action - The ongoing dinner is interrupted by the arrival of the guests.
Action in Progress - The study session is the main action, ongoing during the night.
Background Information - The rain sets a continuous backdrop for the night.
Exercise 3: Creating Sentences with Past Continuous Tense
Create a sentence using the past continuous tense to describe an interrupted action.

Exercise 4: Combining Sentences Using Past Continuous Tense
Combine the following pairs of sentences into one using the past continuous tense.

I read a book. Then, I fell asleep.
She listened to music. Suddenly, her brother shouted.
Solutions

She was listening to music when suddenly her brother shouted.
These exercises should have given you a clearer understanding and practical application of the past continuous tense. By practicing forming sentences and recognizing the tense's various uses, you can gain greater mastery over this aspect of English grammar.

The English language often presents a multitude of ways to express actions that occurred in the past, with the past continuous and simple past tenses being two primary methods. Understanding the nuanced differences between these two forms of past tenses is crucial for effectively conveying the timing and nature of past events.

The simple past tense is utilized to describe actions that were completed at a specific moment in the past. These actions have no direct link to the present and are seen as finished. This tense does not describe the duration of the action, nor does it indicate anything about what was happening simultaneously. When we say, "I walked to the park," we're simply stating that at some point in the past, the action of walking to the park occurred and was completed.

The past continuous tense unfurls a rich tapestry of ongoing actions stitched into the fabric of bygone moments. It's akin to a gentle river of activity, flowing through the temporal landscape, and is crafted linguistically by coupling the past form of the verb 'to be' (embodied as 'was' or 'were') with the verb's present participle, which dons the '-ing' suffix.

Let us explore the realm of this tense through its utilization:

For actions that were unfurling their wings at a distinct slice of yesteryear.
For painting the broad strokes of background activities, which were gently nudged aside by sudden events.
Delve into the heart of these uses with illustrative examples and brain-teasing exercises.

Employment 1: Painting a Past Action with a Temporal Brush
Example: Conjure an image from the annals of the prior eve. You might articulate, "While the clock hands aligned at 8 p.m. last evening, I found myself immersed in the literary world of a novel." Here, the act of reading wasn't a fleeting moment but an ongoing experience at that specific juncture.

Now, let us translate this into a stimulating exercise:

Rewrite Exercise 1: Transform the following scenarios into sentences that reflect the past continuous tense, infusing creativity and uniqueness.

At yesterday's twilight, the pages of a novel (to turn) under the curious eyes of the reader.
As dawn's first light broke, a solitary figure (to jog) along the silent streets.
Creative Solutions:

As yesterday's twilight deepened, the novel's pages were turning under the reader's captivated gaze.
With the arrival of dawn's first light, a solitary figure was found jogging along the whispering streets.
The elegance of the past continuous tense is in its ability to animate the past, setting scenes in motion and infusing narratives with a sense of the perpetual 'now' that once was. It's like watching a silent film where the actions, though quiet, are full of movement and life, allowing the audience to

feel the rhythm of past activities as if they were unfolding before their very eyes.

Exercise 1: Create sentences using the past continuous tense to describe what you were doing at these exact times yesterday:

At 7 a.m.:
At 12 p.m.:
At 6 p.m.:
Solutions to Exercise 1:

At 7 a.m., I was jogging in the park.
At 12 p.m., I was eating lunch with a friend.
At 6 p.m., I was driving home from work.
Use 2: Background Action Interrupted by Another Action
Example: You can use the past continuous to set the scene for another action.

Exercise 2: Write sentences in which the following actions interrupt the background activities. Use the past continuous for the background activity and simple past for the interrupting action:

Background Activity: watching TV
Interrupting Action: a loud noise outside
Solution to Exercise 2:

I was watching TV when a loud noise outside startled me. Now, let's delve deeper into the structure and usage of the past continuous tense with a focus on more technical aspects and rare knowledge content.

Structure of Past Continuous Tense
Technically, the structure of past continuous consists of the subject, the past tense of the verb 'to be' (was/were), and the base verb with an -ing ending. The formula is: Subject + was/were + base verb+ing.

Example: "She was studying all night for the exams."

Exercise 3: Form past continuous sentences using the following subjects and verbs:

Subject: The children / Verb: play
Subject: He / Verb: work
Subject: The artists / Verb: paint
Solutions to Exercise 3:

The children were playing in the garden.
He was working on his new project.
The artists were painting a mural.
Rare Knowledge Content
A less commonly known use of the past continuous is to express a repeated action in the past, which often annoyed the speaker. This is usually accompanied by words like 'always' or 'constantly.'

Exercise 4: Write sentences using past continuous tense to express annoyance about these habits:

Subject: My neighbor / Habit: play loud music late at night
Subject: My cat / Habit: scratch the furniture
Solutions to Exercise 4:

My cat was constantly scratching the furniture.
Practical Applications
In practical situations, such as storytelling or giving background information during conversations, the past continuous tense adds depth and interest to the narrative.

Exercise 5: Create a short story using past continuous tense to describe the setting or background actions. Incorporate at least three past continuous sentences.

Sample Solution to Exercise 5:
While the gentle wind was rustling the leaves, a group of hikers was making their way through the dense woods. Owls were hooting from their hidden perches, creating an eerie

melody. In the midst of this tranquil scene, the hikers were sharing stories of their past adventures.

In summary, the past continuous tense serves not just as a grammatical tool but as a paintbrush to color the canvas of our conversations and writings with the hues of time and motion. Its practice can deepen your understanding of English narrative structure, making your speech and writing richer and more engaging.

Chapter 7: The Past Perfect Tense

The past perfect tense in English grammar is a rather intriguing aspect to explore. It functions as a sort of time machine, allowing us to travel back from a past moment to an even earlier time. It tells us not just what happened, but also the sequence of events. Let's embark on a journey through the past perfect tense, delving into its definition, usage, and the vivid landscapes it can paint in the realm of language.

At its core, the past perfect tense is used to express an action that was completed before another action took place in the past. It's like telling a story within a story, where the main story is in the past, and the past perfect tense is used to flash back to events that happened even earlier.

For example, imagine a finished painting. The action of painting is in the past, but before this masterpiece was complete, there was a moment where the artist first envisioned it. This initial vision is what we express using the past perfect tense: "The artist had envisioned the painting before they began to work on the canvas."

Now, let's unravel the structure of this tense. The past perfect is formed using 'had' followed by the past participle of the verb. The past participle is often – though not always – formed by adding '-ed' to the base verb. However, English is known for its exceptions, and there are many verbs with irregular past participles that one must memorize. For example, the past participle of "write" is "written," not "writed."

In usage, the past perfect tense might appear less frequently than the simple past tense, but it has its own special place. It helps us to create clarity about what happened first when we talk about the past. This is particularly useful in storytelling, where the sequence of events is crucial to understand the narrative. Take this instance: "By the time the audience arrived, the play had already started." The past perfect tense 'had started' indicates that the start of the play preceded the arrival of the audience.

Beyond storytelling, the past perfect tense is also employed in reported speech, when relaying conversations that occurred in the past. For example, "She said she had never seen such a magnificent sunset before." Here, 'had never seen' indicates that her experience of not seeing a magnificent sunset happened before the moment she spoke about it.

In academic writing, the past perfect tense serves to provide background information for past research or events.

Let's craft some exercises to apply the past perfect tense and then solve them to solidify our understanding:

Before the concert began, the band _____ (to set up) all their equipment.
She _____ (to finish) her homework by the time her favorite show started.
They _____ (to eat) by the time we arrived at the party.
Convert the following sentences to past perfect tense:

The birds flew away.
He completed the project.
I read the book.
Combine the following pairs of sentences into one using the past perfect tense:

I made tea. Then I realized there was no milk.
The children went to bed. Then the power went out.
She sold her car. Later, she regretted it.
Fill in the blanks with the past perfect form of the verbs in parentheses:

She had finished (finish) her homework by the time her favorite show started.

They had eaten (eat) by the time we arrived at the party.
Convert the following sentences to past perfect tense:

The birds had flown away.
He had completed the project.
I had read the book.
Combine the following pairs of sentences into one using the past perfect tense:

I had made tea when I realized there was no milk.
The children had gone to bed when the power went out.
She had sold her car when she later regretted it.
Through these exercises, it becomes evident how the past perfect tense allows us to navigate the complexities of time in the stories we tell. Its beauty lies in the layer it adds to our understanding, revealing not just actions, but their echoes through time. This exploration into the past perfect tense demonstrates that grammar is not just a set of rules, but a tool for painting vivid pictures with words, providing clarity, and enhancing the storytelling experience.

   The past perfect tense in English is a verb tense used to indicate that an action was completed (or "perfect") before another action in the past. It is formed using the past tense of the auxiliary verb "to have" (which is "had") followed by the past participle of the main verb.

Let's embark on an explorative journey through the construction of affirmative, negative, and interrogative sentences in the past perfect tense, using examples and exercises to fully grasp their form and function.

Affirmative Sentences in Past Perfect Tense
In an affirmative sentence, we state that something had happened or had been the case. The structure for affirmative sentences in past perfect tense is:

Subject + had + past participle of the verb.

For instance, consider the verb "to finish."

Simple Past: "She finished her work."
Past Perfect: "She had finished her work."
This implies that at some past moment, the action of finishing the work was already complete.

Creative Illustration:
Imagine a grand library with countless books. Each book represents an action, and they are stacked in chronological order, with the most recent on the top. The past perfect tense is like taking a volume from the middle of the stack, showing that it was there, completed, even before the recent ones were placed on top.

Sample Exercise:
Create an affirmative past perfect sentence using the verb "to paint."
Solution:
Negative Sentences in Past Perfect Tense
Negative sentences in the past perfect tense are used to describe that something had not been completed before another past action took place. The structure is:

Subject + had not + past participle of the verb.

For example, with the verb "to eat":

Creative Illustration:
Envision a painter with a blank canvas. He plans to paint a sky full of stars. In past perfect negative, we are essentially saying that the sky had not yet been painted with stars by the time night fell. The canvas remained untouched, and the stars were not present on it before a specific moment in the past.

Sample Exercise:
Construct a negative past perfect sentence with the verb "to decide."

Solution:
Interrogative Sentences in Past Perfect Tense
Interrogative sentences in the past perfect tense are used to ask if an action had been completed before another past event. The structure is:

Had + subject + past participle of the verb?

So, with the verb "to leave":

Simple Past: "Did you leave the party early?"
Past Perfect: "Had you left the party before midnight?"
This questions whether the person was no longer at the party when midnight struck.

Creative Illustration:
Think of time as a river and each past action as a boat on that river. When we form interrogative sentences in past perfect, we are asking if a particular boat (action) had already sailed past a certain point on the river (a moment in time) before another boat was seen.

Sample Exercise:
Formulate an interrogative sentence using the past perfect tense with the verb "to read."
Concluding Creative Narrative:
To tie all this together, let's imagine a time traveler's diary written in past perfect tense. The traveler ventures through history, and their diary notes whether actions were completed before others. The affirmative statements confirm their achievements ("I had visited ancient Egypt before I went to medieval Europe"), the negative declare what they missed ("I had not seen the pyramids before I left for Greece"), and the interrogative questions probe the order of their experiences ("Had I learned Latin before I conversed with Caesar?").

Practice Exercise Set:
Now, let's create a mini-test for you to strengthen your understanding of the past perfect tense:

Write an affirmative past perfect sentence with the verb "to lock."

Construct a negative past perfect sentence with the verb "to meet."

Solution: "Had you understood the importance of the discovery before it was explained?"
By applying these structures, you can create a vivid picture of events and their sequence in the past, which is particularly useful in storytelling, academic writing, and everyday conversation. Through regular practice, the formation of these sentences in past perfect tense will become second nature.

   Understanding the past perfect tense in English is crucial for expressing actions that were completed before a specific point in the past, constructing reported speech accurately, and discussing hypothetical situations. This tense enriches our storytelling, making it clearer when certain events happened in relation to others.

"She had finished her work before the deadline." This sentence indicates that the action of finishing occurred before another action or time in the past, which is the deadline.

Imagine a timeline where every event is a point. The past perfect tense allows us to describe an event that is further back on the timeline than another past event.

Let's delve into various scenarios where the past perfect tense is appropriate, and then explore exercises to apply this knowledge practically.

Hypothetical Situations:

Hypothetical situations often occur in conditional sentences, specifically in the third conditional. These are situations that did not happen in the past, but we imagine what the result would have been if they had occurred. For instance, "If I had known you were in town, I would have called you." Here, 'had known' is in the past perfect tense and reflects an event that did not happen — my knowing you were in town.

Reported Speech:

When it comes to reported speech, the past perfect tense allows us to express what someone said without changing the original meaning, even if we are reporting it at a much later time. If your friend says, "I lost my keys," and you tell someone else about it the next day, you would say, "She said she had lost her keys." The use of 'had lost' indicates that the losing of the keys happened before the reporting.

Before Specific Times or Actions in the Past:

This is perhaps the most straightforward use of the past perfect tense. It sets the scene for what had happened up until another action took place. For example, "By the time the party started, I had already gone home." The action of going home is completed before the party started.

Now, let's get creative and explore these uses through sample exercises, incorporating a mixture of sentence structures and paragraph lengths.

Exercise 1: Story Completion

Imagine a short story that begins with the following sentences:

It was much later than she had thought, and the streets were deserted."

Complete the story using at least five sentences in the past perfect tense, ensuring that the actions described by this tense are logically positioned before the events already mentioned.

Sample Answer to Exercise 1:

Maria had always prided herself on her punctuality, so realizing she had stayed late was unsettling. She had planned to leave the office by 5 PM, but an unexpected meeting had extended far beyond the scheduled time. By the time she had wrapped up the last email, darkness had cloaked the city in its quietude. She remembered she had agreed to meet her friend for dinner, but that promise was now as empty as the streets before her. Her stomach rumbled, a reminder that she had skipped lunch in the rush of her tasks.

Exercise 2: Conditional Sentences Creation

Create five sentences using the third conditional. Each sentence should describe a hypothetical situation in the past and its possible outcome.

Sample Answer to Exercise 2:

If I had studied harder, I might have passed the exam with distinction.
Had we known about the traffic jam, we could have taken an alternative route.
If she had set her alarm, she wouldn't have missed the flight.
They would have been here by now if they hadn't missed the train.
If he had saved his document, he wouldn't have lost all his work when the computer crashed.

Exercise 3: Reported Speech Conversion

Convert the following direct speech sentences into reported speech using the past perfect tense where necessary.

"I bought a new car," said John.
"She finished the project," Susan claimed.
"They had never been to Asia before," remarked the couple.
Sample Answer to Exercise 3:

John mentioned that he had bought a new car.
They informed me that they had gone to the cinema the night before.
He admitted that he hadn't seen her at the party.
Susan claimed that she had finished the project.
The couple remarked that they had never been to Asia before.
Through these exercises, we can see the practical applications of the past perfect tense. It's essential in formal writing to convey time relationships clearly, maintain the integrity of reported speech, and to discuss events that are counterfactual.

The past perfect and simple past tenses are two ways we talk about things that happened before now, but they do different jobs in a sentence. Let's embark on an explorative journey to distinguish these two aspects of English storytelling.

The simple past tense is like a snapshot. It's used to describe actions that started and finished at a specific time in the past. When you say, "I walked to the park," you're telling someone that at some point in the past, you went for a walk, and you completed that action. It's straightforward and one of the most common ways to recount past events.

Now, imagine you're layering stories, one over the other. This is where the past perfect comes into play. It's a bit like a flashback in a movie, used to talk about an action that was completed before another action in the past. If you say, "I had walked to the park," it implies that the walk was completed before another past event you are thinking about. It's as if you're setting the scene for something that happened after this walk.

Let's delve into a practical application. Picture two friends, Anne and Bob, who planned to meet yesterday. Anne arrived at the meeting point at 2 PM and waited. Bob arrived at 3 PM. Describing this scenario in simple past, we might say, "Anne arrived at 2 PM. Bob arrived at 3 PM." We've got two snapshots, simple and clear. But what if Anne is telling the story? She could say, "I had arrived at the meeting point when Bob came." Now, Anne's arrival is given a sense of being further back in time, setting the stage for Bob's later arrival.

In storytelling, the past perfect is like a brush that paints depth, allowing us to see the order of events clearly. Suppose a character in a book is reflecting on their life. The author might use the past perfect to show what the character had done in their youth before moving to the simple past to bring the reader back to the main timeline of events.

Let's craft a sample scenario to exercise our understanding:

Imagine Sarah is writing a diary about her weekend adventure. She visited a castle and later lost her phone. Here's how she might use the tenses:

Simple Past:
Yesterday was eventful. I visited an old castle in the morning. The view from the top was breathtaking. In the afternoon, I realized I lost my phone.

Past Perfect:
Yesterday was eventful. When I realized my phone was missing, I remembered I had taken many photos at the castle. I had left the castle before I noticed the phone was gone. I wondered if I had dropped it there.

In the first narrative, events are simply listed. In the second, the past perfect sets up a timeline, showing Sarah had enjoyed her visit and taken photos, all of which happened before the unfortunate realization of her lost phone.

Understanding the difference can be pivotal. For instance, in legal or historical documents, clarity about the sequence of events can affect the interpretation of the information. A historian, for instance, would be careful to say, "The king had signed the treaty before the war ended," ensuring that readers understand the signing happened earlier.

In the everyday world, these tenses help us communicate more effectively. If you're explaining why you were late, you could say, "The bus had already left when I got to the station," instead of, "I was late because the bus left."

Now, let's try solving a problem using both tenses:

Problem:
Laura forgot to send an email. She remembered it only after her boss asked about it the next day.

Simple Past Solution:
Yesterday, Laura forgot to send an email. Today, her boss asked her about it, and she remembered.

Past Perfect Solution:
Laura had forgotten to send an email by the time her boss inquired about it today, prompting her memory.

By using the past perfect, we've demonstrated that Laura's action of forgetting happened before the subsequent action of her boss asking.

To sum it up, the past perfect sets the stage for another past event, providing context and a timeline, while the simple past just tells us what happened, plain and simple. Both are integral in crafting rich, detailed past narratives, whether in casual conversation, professional communication, or creative writing. The depth and clarity of past events are often best expressed through the interplay of these two tenses, painting a vivid picture of the sequence in which things have occurred.

The past perfect tense in English is used to describe an action that was completed before another action or time in the past. It is formed by using 'had' followed by the past participle of the verb.

Let's embark on an explorative journey into the world of the past perfect tense, weaving through its intricacies with examples and crafted exercises that are both innovative and instructive.

Understanding the Past Perfect Tense
Imagine you are peering through the window of time, looking back at events that have concluded before a certain moment in the past. That's where the past perfect tense comes into play, allowing you to clarify the sequence of past events.

For example, consider two past events: John ate dinner, and John went to the movies. If John ate dinner before he went to the movies, and you want to talk about it after both have happened, you could say, "John had eaten dinner before he went to the movies." This sentence uses the past perfect tense to show that eating dinner occurred first.

Delving into Creativity with Past Perfect
To master the past perfect tense, let's weave its usage into creative contexts:

Story-Telling Exercise:
Craft a short story using the past perfect tense to indicate actions completed before others.

Story Prompt: Once in a quaint village, a curious cat named Whiskers had embarked on a secret mission.

Story Exercise:
Whiskers had always been an adventurous feline, but this time, he had bitten off more than he could chew. Before the night fell, Whiskers had already deciphered the ancient map

he found in the attic. The map had promised treasures buried beneath the old oak tree, which had stood in the village square for centuries. Whiskers had decided that the treasure was his to claim. He had packed his tiny backpack with all the necessary tools before the village clock struck ten. Little did he know, Mrs. Paws, the mayor's cat, had been watching him with keen eyes and had planned to follow him.

Reflection: This exercise uses the past perfect tense to indicate actions that Whiskers completed before other events in the past.

Interactive Exercises
Conversation Recreation:
Rewrite a conversation using the past perfect tense to show what each person had done earlier.

Original Conversation:

Person A: "I called you earlier."
Person B: "I was at the store."
Person C: "I saw your car there."
Recreated Conversation:

Person A: "I had called you earlier."
Person B: "I had gone to the store."
Person C: "I had seen your car there."
Reflection: This recreation helps you practice transforming simple past statements into past perfect tense.

Diary Entry Exercise:
Write a diary entry about your day using the past perfect tense to describe events that were completed earlier.

Diary Prompt: Reflect on a busy day you had last week.
Diary Exercise:
Dear Diary,
Last week had been particularly bustling for me. By the time I sat down for dinner, I had completed three different

projects. My colleagues had left for the day, unaware that I had resolved the issue with the server. Before the lunch hour had arrived, I had already attended four meetings and had prepared the documents for the next day. I had hoped to leave early, but as fate had it, I had been caught up with unexpected tasks until dusk.

Reflection: This exercise helps to incorporate the past perfect tense into personal narratives, showcasing how events fit into a broader timeline.

Sequence of Events Exercise:
Create sentences that describe a sequence of events, using the past perfect tense for actions that occurred first.

Sequence Prompt: Planning a surprise party, baking a cake, guests arriving.

Sequence Exercise:

By the time the guests had arrived, I had already planned the entire surprise party.
I had baked the cake before they had even knocked on the door.
After everyone had settled in, we revealed the surprise, but I had been preparing for this moment all week long.
Reflection: The past perfect tense in these sentences emphasizes the preparation that was completed before the guests came.

Summative Exercises
Error Correction:
Identify and correct the past perfect tense errors in the paragraph below.

Error-Laden Paragraph:
By the time we reached the airport, the plane leave. I had think that we had left the house early enough. She tell me she had set the alarm, but we had oversleep.

Corrected Paragraph:
By the time we reached the airport, the plane had left. I had thought that we had left the house early enough. She told me she had set the alarm, but we had overslept.

Reflection: Correcting these sentences gives you an opportunity to reinforce your understanding of the structure of the past perfect tense.

Creative Description:
Describe a historical event using the past perfect tense to establish the timeline of occurrences.

Historical Event: The Moon Landing in 1969.

Creative Description:
Before humanity had taken its first steps on the Moon, scientists and astronauts had worked tirelessly for years. They had developed technology that had never existed before. When Neil Armstrong had planted his foot on the lunar surface, the world had already witnessed a series of groundbreaking advances. The Apollo 11 crew had trained for scenarios more challenging than any before, and they had overcome countless obstacles to reach this unprecedented moment in history.

Reflection: This exercise lets you apply the past perfect tense to real-world events, thereby understanding its practical utility in giving context to historical sequences.

Through these exercises, we've journeyed across narrative landscapes, historical vistas, and everyday dialogues, employing the past perfect tense to clarify the chronology of past events. The creative application of this tense enhances both the clarity and richness of language expression, making it an indispensable tool in the craft of storytelling and the relay of information.

Chapter 8: The Simple Future Tense

The simple future tense is a verb form used to discuss something that hasn't happened yet but will occur later. In English, it's often constructed with "will" followed by the base form of a verb, such as "will eat" or "will go." Sometimes, especially in conversational English, "shall" replaces "will" for the first person (I and we), though it's more formal and much less common in modern English.

For instance, if you plan to go to the market later, you would say, "I will go to the market." This indicates a future action. The simplicity of the simple future tense makes it a fundamental aspect of English language learning, as it allows speakers to easily discuss plans, predictions, and promises.

The usage of the simple future tense stretches across various contexts. Let's explore these in detail, each accompanied by creative examples and sample exercises.

Predictions
We often use the simple future tense to make predictions about the future. These predictions are not guaranteed to happen but are seen as likely based on current evidence or beliefs.

Example: "It will rain tomorrow." – Here, the speaker believes that there is a high chance of rain based on, perhaps, a weather report or dark clouds in the sky.

Promises
Promises are commitments that one will do something in the future, and the simple future tense is perfect for expressing these commitments.

Voluntary Actions
When someone decides to do something at the moment of speaking, without previous planning, the simple future tense is used.

Offers
We use the simple future tense to offer to do something for someone else.

Example: "I will make you some coffee." – This suggests the speaker is offering to prepare coffee for someone else.

Decisions
When a decision is made at the moment of speaking, the simple future tense comes into play.

Example: "I think I will go for a walk now." – The speaker decides to go for a walk just at that moment.

Assumptions
The simple future tense is used when assuming something about the present or future.

Example: "They will be home by now." – The speaker assumes that "they" have already reached home.

Now, let's create a sample exercise to apply the simple future tense:

Exercise: Complete the sentences with the simple future tense of the verbs in parentheses.

I _____ (finish) the report by tomorrow.
She _____ (start) her new job next week.
They _____ (celebrate) their anniversary next month.
We _____ (plan) the event once we get the approval.
The sky is dark; it _____ (rain) soon.
Answers:

I will finish the report by tomorrow.
She will start her new job next week.
They will celebrate their anniversary next month.
We will plan the event once we get the approval.
The sky is dark; it will rain soon.

Practical Applications

Understanding and correctly using the simple future tense is invaluable in everyday communication, whether in planning events, setting goals, or making arrangements. In professional settings, it facilitates clear and effective planning and scheduling. For example, a manager might say to their team, "We will meet every Monday to track the project's progress."

In personal contexts, the simple future can express intentions and dreams, like when a child says, "I will become an astronaut." It's also instrumental in creating a respectful atmosphere when making offers or promises, which strengthens relationships and builds trust.

In conclusion, the simple future tense is an essential aspect of English that enables people to express intentions, predictions, and plans with clarity and simplicity. Its versatility makes it applicable in a myriad of situations, making it a crucial tool for communication in both personal and professional contexts. By practicing the creation of sentences using this tense, one can master its use and thereby become more adept at articulating future-related concepts.

Creating sentences in the simple future tense involves a dance with time, a projection into what is yet to unfold. In its essence, the simple future tense is employed when we wish to speak of events that have not yet occurred, but will at some point beyond the present. To craft sentences in the simple future tense, we typically use the auxiliary verb "will" followed by the base form of the main verb.

To convey a sense of affirmation, where we state that something will indeed happen, we use the affirmative form. For instance, "She will travel to Paris next month." Here, 'will travel' indicates a certainty about the future action.

When we step into the realm of negation, expressing that something will not take place, we insert 'not' after 'will'. For example, "He will not attend the meeting tomorrow." The contraction 'won't' can also be used as in "He won't attend the meeting tomorrow."

Questions about the future, posed to seek information or clarification, make use of the interrogative form. Here, 'will' comes before the subject, as in "Will you join us for dinner?"

Let us now look at these forms through the lens of creative examples, shall we?

Affirmative Sentences in the Simple Future Tense

The sun will rise from the east, painting the sky with strokes of orange and pink, heralding a new day.
Willows by the river will sway in the forthcoming spring breeze, their leaves whispering secrets to the waters below.
Children in the park will laugh with unbridled joy, their merry voices carrying the timeless tune of play and freedom.
Books will continue to be silent companions, offering worlds trapped between their covers, waiting to be discovered.
Innovations in technology will unfold, stretching the canvas of human capability further into the realms of the unknown.
Negative Sentences in the Simple Future Tense

The ancient oak tree will not yield to the storm; it will stand tall, its roots grasping the earth with the strength of centuries.
Wisdom will not come hastily to the impatient; it prefers the quiet contemplation of the persistent seeker.
The secrets of the deep sea will not unveil themselves easily; they require the persistent curiosity of the daring.
The stars will not falter in their nightly journey across the heavens; they are the timeless voyagers of the celestial sea.
Our dreams will not diminish with the passing of seasons; they are the seeds that will grow with each nurturing thought.

Interrogative Sentences in the Simple Future Tense

Will the poet's words find a home in the hearts of those
yearning for solace?
Will the melody of the ancient flute still float across the
village square when twilight descends?
Will humanity find a way to heal the scars it has etched upon
the earth?
Will the whisper of the autumn leaves still carry the stories
of the old days to those who listen closely?
Will the dance of the northern lights continue to cast its spell
upon the arctic night?
Sample Exercise for Practicing Simple Future Tense

Let's engage in a creative exercise to solidify our
understanding of the simple future tense. Below is a short
paragraph with blanks to fill in with the appropriate form of
the simple future tense, whether affirmative, negative, or
interrogative.

In the city of tomorrow, buildings (1) _____ (to rise) high
into the sky, like fingers stretching for the stars. Pollution (2)
_____ (not/to choke) the air, for technology (3) _____ (to
bring) forth solutions for clean energy. People (4) _____ (to
walk) or (5) _____ (to cycle) to work, with cars becoming
relics of a bygone era. The question remains, (6) _____
(society/to embrace) these changes willingly?

Solutions:

will rise
will not choke
will bring
will walk
will cycle
will society embrace
By employing the simple future tense, we paint images of
what's to come, engage with the potential of tomorrow, and
explore the mysteries that the future holds. It's a linguistic

tool that allows us to dream and plan, to wonder and to warn. The beauty of the future tense lies in its inherent optimism: the belief in the continuation of time and the unfolding of events yet to be witnessed.

Understanding the simple future tense is essential for conveying events that have not yet occurred but are expected or planned to happen. It's a verb tense often used for making predictions, promises, and expressing spontaneous decisions. The structure typically involves the auxiliary "will" followed by the base form of the main verb. Now, let's dive deep into its use for predictions, promises, and spontaneous decisions with a variety of examples and explanations.

Predictions

Predictions are statements about what someone believes will happen in the future. In the simple future tense, these often take the form of "will" plus the verb. For instance:
"The weatherman said it will rain tomorrow." Here, we're expressing a forecast about the weather based on information from a reliable source.
"Given the current trends, it is likely that the world's population will reach 9 billion by 2050." This prediction is based on existing trends and data analysis.
"The movie starts at 8 PM, so it will probably be over by 10 PM." This is a prediction based on the typical length of movies.
Here's an exercise to practice predictions: Think about a technological innovation and predict how it might change our lives in the future. Write five sentences using the simple future tense.
Sample Prediction Exercise:

"3D printers will be common in homes, allowing people to manufacture everyday items on-demand."
"Telemedicine will revolutionize healthcare by providing remote diagnostics and treatments."

"Virtual reality will transform education, making learning experiences more interactive and immersive."
"Artificial intelligence will simplify complex decision-making, leading to more efficient business processes."
Promises

Promises are commitments that one makes about what they intend to do in the future. They often take a very personal tone and imply a sense of responsibility and intent.
"I will always be there for you." This is a deep personal commitment to someone else.
"You will receive your refund within two weeks." This is a business promise to a customer.
Here's an exercise for promises: Write down five promises that you would make to improve your community using the simple future tense.
Sample Promise Exercise:

"I will start a community garden to promote sustainable living among my neighbors."
Spontaneous Decisions

Spontaneous decisions are made at the moment of speaking, without pre-planning or forethought. They often occur in reaction to something or as a quick resolve.
"Oh, I forgot to call Sarah.
"It's getting cold in here. I will turn up the heat." This decision is made because of the sudden realization of the cold.
"You look tired. I will make dinner tonight." Here, the speaker decides to help someone upon noticing their fatigue.
"We're out of coffee?
"This charity is doing great work. I will make a donation." The decision to donate is made spontaneously after learning about the charity's work.
Here's an exercise for spontaneous decisions: Imagine you are at a friend's house for dinner and several things happen that require quick action. Write five sentences using the simple future tense to show your spontaneous decisions.

Sample Spontaneous Decision Exercise:

"The baby is crying; I will go check on her."
"It seems we need more chairs; I will fetch a few from the garage."
"You've spilled your drink; I will get a cloth to clean it up."

The art of peering into tomorrow through the lens of language is a fascinating study of how we shape our expectations and intentions. English unfurls this anticipation through not just one, but several tenses, each a different hue on the palette of futurity. The simple future tense, present continuous, future continuous, future perfect, and future perfect continuous: these are the tools with which English paints tomorrow's potentialities.

Embarking on the Simple Future

When we turn our gaze towards events yet to unfurl, we often employ the simple future tense. It's akin to planting a flag in the terrain of time, declaring, "Here, an action shall rise." We forge this simple future with the auxiliary "will," followed by the unadorned verb, much like:

"I will dine when the clock strikes seven."
In this crystal-clear proclamation, there's an action lying in wait, ready to emerge at a destined moment. It's intention set forth plainly, a beacon in the yet-to-be.

Other Temporal Canvases

Venture we now to the realms that are mapped out with greater intricacy, with futures that twist and turn in varied spirals:

Present Continuous with an Eye on Tomorrow
Imagine a string tied from the present to a pin in the calendar of the coming days; this is the present continuous speaking of the future—a testament to plans cast in stone:

"Tomorrow's dawn shall find me at the meeting with a friend."
This sentence is more than a simple future marker; it's a promise, a plan with its roots deep in the certainty of now.

Future Continuous: A Brush Stroke Over Time
Consider a painting where a moment is stretched, a scene in motion under the sky of someday; this is the essence of the future continuous tense. It flows like a river through "will be" cascading into the ongoing "-ing" form:

Here, we capture a snapshot of a future in motion, an act caught midway through its performance.

Future Perfect: The Art of Conclusion
Now, let's envision a timeline, with a dot marking the full stop of an act; this is the domain of the future perfect tense. It is sculpted using "will have" plus the verb's past participle:

In this, we focus on the finale, the future point where an action reaches its denouement.

Future Perfect Continuous: Weaving Duration into Destiny
Lastly, imagine an hourglass with sand flowing, not to run out, but to mark the stretch of action up to and beyond a point in the forthcoming times. The future perfect continuous tense wraps this concept in "will have been" followed by the verb's "-ing" form:

Here, the duration is king, the continuity and the unbroken chain of action are the soul of the sentence.
Exercise in Temporal Artistry
Let us paint a scenario with these tenses to witness the rich tapestry they create.

Envision the preparations for a festivity in your garden. You can depict the nuances of your anticipation with the various tenses:

Future Continuous:

"Under next week's sun, in the midst of laughter and conversation, will I be."
Each sentence weaves a layer of foresight, crafting a full-bodied vision of the celebration to come.

To conclude, while the simple future lays out a singular thread of intent or forecast, the other forms interweave complexities of arrangements, the flux of activities, the endpoints of endeavors, and the span of engagements as they relate to the morrow. The kaleidoscope of these tenses enriches not merely the chronology of forthcoming events but also embroiders the fabric of our perceptions and sentiments about them. To grasp and to wield these forms is to hold a painter's brush, with which one can color the canvas of communication in English with both precision and depth.

Understanding and mastering the simple future tense in English can be both engaging and educational. This tense is utilized to express an action that is predicted or expected to happen in the future. Here are some examples and exercises to deepen your understanding.

Examples of Simple Future Tense
The Sky's Predictions:

Tonight, the meteorologists predict that the stars will shine brighter after midnight.
As the hours pass, the moon will climb higher, and its light will bathe the landscape in a silver glow.
Technology's Leap:

In the next decade, innovators will unlock new potentials in artificial intelligence.
Smartphones will evolve beyond our current understanding, becoming even more integrated into our daily lives.

Nature's Course:
Come spring, the cherry blossoms will unfurl their pink petals against the city's skyline.
The dormant seeds beneath the soil will awaken and soon, they will sprout into a vibrant tapestry of colors.
Human Aspirations:

Tomorrow, thousands of students around the world will take a step closer to their dreams as they apply for college.
In years to come, many of these young minds will lead the charge in innovative solutions to global challenges.
Unfolding Stories:

By the end of the book, the protagonist will have encountered numerous challenges, shaping her into a true heroine.
The plot will twist again, surprising readers with an unexpected turn of events.
Exercises on Simple Future Tense
Exercise 1: Predict the Future
Imagine you are a futurist. Write five sentences predicting what the world of technology will look like in 2050. Use the simple future tense.

Sample Exercise:

In 2050, robots will perform the majority of household chores.
Virtual reality will become an everyday escape for millions.
Cars will no longer require drivers, as they will navigate themselves.
Personal assistants will not only be digital but also anticipate needs before being expressed.
Quantum computers will solve complex problems in seconds that currently take days.

Exercise 2: Plan an Event
Create an invitation for a future event using the simple future tense to describe five different activities or highlights that will take place.
Sample Exercise:

Next Saturday, at our annual community picnic, the local band will play live music from noon until sunset.
The children will participate in a treasure hunt that will take them on an adventure around the park.
Local chefs will prepare a feast that will tantalize your taste buds.
Artists will display their work, offering a glimpse into the creative soul of our community.
As the day concludes, we will launch lanterns into the night sky, symbolizing our shared hopes and dreams.
Exercise 3: New Year's Resolutions
Write down five resolutions for the next year using the simple future tense.

Sample Exercise:

I will dedicate an hour each day to learning a new language.
I will start a daily journal to document my thoughts and experiences.
I will commit to a healthier lifestyle by incorporating exercise into my routine.
I will read at least one book a month to expand my horizons.
I will volunteer my time every month to help those in need within my community.
Exercise 4: Weather Forecast
Pretend you are a weather forecaster. Write a forecast for the week ahead using the simple future tense.

Sample Exercise:

Tomorrow, the sun will rise to a clear sky, with temperatures soaring to new highs.

By midweek, clouds will gather, and we will likely see some rain showers.

Thursday will bring a cool breeze, which will lower the temperatures slightly.

The weekend will offer a respite as the weather will become mild and pleasant.

Sunday evening will close the week with the possibility of a thunderstorm.

Exercise 5: A Letter to Your Future Self

Compose a letter to yourself 10 years from now. Use the simple future tense to describe where you will be, what you will be doing, and how you will feel about the changes around you.

Sample Exercise:

In ten years, I will be living in a city that fosters innovation and creativity.

By that time, I will have achieved my goal of becoming an expert in renewable energy sources.

I will be mentoring the next generation of leaders, sharing my experiences and knowledge.

Technology will have advanced, but I will remain committed to personal connections.

I am confident that I will look back on the past decade with pride and a sense of accomplishment.

By engaging in these exercises, you will not only reinforce your understanding of the simple future tense but also stretch your imagination and writing skills. The simple future tense opens up a world of possibilities, allowing you to express hopes, predictions, and plans with clarity and confidence.

Chapter 9: The Future Continuous Tense

The future continuous tense, also known as the future progressive tense, is used to describe actions that will be in progress at a specific moment in the future. It allows us to envision a future scenario where a particular activity is unfolding over time. This tense is formed using the auxiliary verbs "will be" followed by the present participle of the main verb (the -ing form).

To illustrate the future continuous tense, imagine painting a picture. The action is not instant; it takes time and extends over a duration. Now, if you plan to be doing this activity tomorrow at a certain time, you are looking ahead to that period when you'll be in the middle of painting. That's the essence of the future continuous tense.

Here's how you can construct sentences using the future continuous tense:

Affirmative: Subject + will be + present participle (-ing form)

Example: "Tomorrow at noon, I will be painting a portrait."
Negative: Subject + will not be + present participle (-ing form)

Example:
Interrogative: Will + subject + be + present participle (-ing form)?

Example: "Will you be using the conference room this time tomorrow?"
The future continuous tense serves several practical applications. For one, it helps in expressing future plans or actions in a more dynamic way, indicating the continuity of the action. It's also useful for polite inquiries about

someone's plans without the directness of a simple future tense. Additionally, it can be employed to predict the present, such as guessing what someone might be doing right now.

Sample Exercise:

Imagine you are planning a series of events for a day next week. Write down five activities you anticipate will be happening at specific times using the future continuous tense.

At 8:00 AM, I will be jogging around the park.
By 10:00 AM, I will be attending a seminar on climate change.
At noon, I will be discussing business strategies with my colleagues.
At 3:00 PM, I will be reviewing the latest market analysis reports.
In the evening, at 7:00 PM, I will be dining with an important client.
Solutions:

The provided sentences are the solutions themselves, showcasing the use of the future continuous tense in planning future activities and indicating the ongoing nature of these events at specific times.

The Future Continuous Tense, often used to describe an action that will be in progress at a certain point in the future, is a valuable aspect of English grammar. Crafting sentences in this tense involves the subject, followed by the appropriate form of the auxiliary verb 'will be,' and the present participle of the main verb (the -ing form).

Affirmative Sentences in Future Continuous Tense
In affirmative sentences, we express a positive action that will be happening at a specific time. Here's the structure:

Subject + will be + present participle of verb + (optional time indicator)

For example:

Tomorrow at this time, I will be traveling to New York.
In this sentence, 'I' is the subject, 'will be traveling' is the verb in its future continuous form, and 'tomorrow at this time' is the time indicator.

'She' is the subject, 'will be waiting' is the future continuous form of the verb 'wait,' and 'when we arrive' indicates the future time.

They will be studying all night for the final exam.
The subject is 'They,' the verb in future continuous form is 'will be studying,' and 'all night for the final exam' gives us the time context.

We will be enjoying the party this weekend.
In this sentence, 'We' is the subject and 'will be enjoying' is the future continuous verb, with 'this weekend' serving as the time frame.

The earth will be completing another rotation in 24 hours.
'The earth' is the subject, 'will be completing' is the verb phrase in future continuous tense, and 'in 24 hours' provides the time element.

Negative Sentences in Future Continuous Tense
To form negative sentences, simply insert 'not' between 'will' and 'be.'

Subject + will not be + present participle of verb + (optional time indicator)

For example:
'I' is the subject, 'will not be going' is the negative future continuous form of 'go,' and 'tomorrow' is the time indicator.

She will not be joining the meeting next week.
The subject 'She,' the negative verb phrase 'will not be joining,' and the time frame 'next week' are present in this sentence.

They will not be working at that time.
In this instance, 'They' is the subject, 'will not be working' is in the future continuous negative form, and 'at that time' tells us when.

We will not be staying late after the event.
'We' is the subject, 'will not be staying' is the verb in the future continuous negative, and 'late after the event' is the time indicator.

The sun will not be shining at midnight.
The subject is 'The sun,' the verb phrase in future continuous negative form is 'will not be shining,' and 'at midnight' gives us the time frame.

Interrogative Sentences in Future Continuous Tense
When asking questions in the future continuous tense, invert the subject and 'will.'

Will + subject + be + present participle of verb + (optional time indicator)?

For example:

Will you be using this computer later?
'Will you be using' is the interrogative form, and 'later' is the time indicator.

Will she be staying with you during her visit?
The sentence begins with the interrogative phrase 'Will she be staying,' and 'during her visit' indicates the time.

Will they be having dinner at the new restaurant tonight?

116

'Will they be having' forms the question, with 'tonight' specifying when.

Will we be meeting the delegates in the main hall?
Here, 'Will we be meeting' is used to ask the question, with 'in the main hall' giving the location context.

Will the earth be facing a significant climate change by the end of the century?
The interrogative phrase 'Will the earth be facing' begins the question, and 'by the end of the century' provides the future time frame.

Sample Exercises and Solutions
Exercise 1: Form an affirmative sentence in the future continuous tense.
Subject: The scientists
Base verb: research
Time indicator: at midnight tonight
Solution: The scientists will be researching at midnight tonight.

Exercise 2: Convert the affirmative sentence to negative.
Affirmative: The musicians will be performing at the festival.
Solution: The musicians will not be performing at the festival.

Exercise 3: Create an interrogative sentence using the future continuous tense.
Subject: The train
Base verb: arrive
Time indicator: by 3 PM
Solution: Will the train be arriving by 3 PM?

Exercise 4: Write an affirmative future continuous sentence about a predicted technological advancement.
Subject: Robots
Base verb: assist

Time indicator: in everyday household tasks
Solution: Robots will be assisting in everyday household
tasks within the next decade.

Exercise 5: Form a negative sentence about a hypothetical
situation.
Subject: People
Base verb: live
Time indicator: on Mars
Solution: People will not be living on Mars by the year 2050,
as some have speculated.

Understanding how to construct sentences in the future
continuous tense allows for more precise and varied
expression, especially when discussing future plans,
predictions, or events that will be in progress at a specific
point in time. Through practice, the formation of these
sentences becomes intuitive, allowing for fluid
communication and a richer language experience.

The future continuous tense is a fascinating aspect of the
English language, woven intricately into the fabric of time
and prediction. It is an essential tense that elegantly bridges
the present with the vibrant tapestry of yet-to-come
moments. Let us explore its utility, its formation, and its
multifaceted applications in the realm of communication and
thought projection.

Firstly, envision the future continuous tense as a temporal
kaleidoscope, where actions are captured in motion, set
against the clock of future time. It's formed with the subject,
followed by the auxiliary verb "will," then the auxiliary verb
"be," and finally the present participle of the main verb (the
"-ing" form). The skeleton of this construction looks like
this: "Subject + will be + present participle."

Consider the sentence: "At this time tomorrow, I will be
sailing across the azure waters." This example illustrates a
snapshot, a scene of action in the process at a specific future

time. It's as if the future continuous tense throws a lasso around an hour or a minute in the days ahead, pulling an ongoing activity into the spotlight of our mind's theater.

The practical applications of this tense are abundant. Let's navigate through different scenarios:

Scheduled Events and Future Plans:
When outlining schedules or discussing future plans, the future continuous underscores the continuity of upcoming events. Imagine an event coordinator speaking to a team: "At 9 AM on Monday, we will be commencing the first session of the conference." It's not just a statement of plan; it's an assurance of action in progression at that moment.

Predictions Based on Evidence:
It's not all about plans and schedules; sometimes, the future continuous acts as a seer's crystal ball. It's used for making predictions when there is some form of present evidence or when something is expected to continue for a certain period. For example, "Given the dark clouds gathering, it looks like it will be raining all evening." The prediction is not wild; it's tethered to the tangible sign of the dark clouds.

Politeness:
Sometimes, the future continuous can soften the edge of inquiry or request, making it sound less immediate and therefore more polite. Asking, "Will you be using the printer soon?" carries a gentler tone than "Will you use the printer?"

To solidify our understanding, let's engage in some sample exercises, shall we?

Exercise 1:
Craft sentences using the future continuous tense for the following scenarios:

a. Describing what someone will be doing at 8 PM tonight based on their current plan.

b. Making a prediction about the state of technology in ten years.

c. Polite inquiry about someone's availability next week.

In literary applications, the future continuous can evoke a sense of foreboding or anticipation. A novelist might write, "By the turn of the century, they will be living in a world far different from our own," to stir the reader's imagination, painting a picture of evolution and change.

Moreover, in the domains of academic and research analysis, where forecasting and trend prediction are essential, this tense offers a nuanced lens. A research analyst might project, "By the third quarter, the company will be implementing the new strategy to increase its market share."

To wield the future continuous tense is to have the deft ability to reach into tomorrow's actions and narrate them with the assuredness of a storyteller. It is a versatile tool in the linguistic kit, serving not only to express certainty about the future but also to convey ongoing action with grace and subtlety.

In conclusion, the future continuous tense is not merely a grammatical construct; it is a dance of time and verb, a leap into the forthcoming with the finesse of linguistic precision. It is as much about the framing of actions within time as it is about the texture of those actions, imbuing them with the essence of continuity, prediction, and sometimes, the soft touch of politeness. Through the examples and exercises we've woven together, the conceptual grasp of the future continuous tense should now be as vivid and actionable as the scenes it describes in the theatre of the future.

The future continuous and simple future tenses in English are both ways to talk about actions that will happen at a later time, but they serve different purposes and convey different nuances about the future events.

Simple Future Tense

The simple future tense is used to describe actions that have not yet occurred but will occur at some point later on. It is often employed when the speaker wants to make a prediction, offer a promise, or express a willingness to do something. The formation is straightforward: you use "will" followed by the base form of the verb for all subjects (I, you, he, she, it, we, they).

For example:

"She will travel to France next year." (Prediction)
"I will finish the report by tomorrow." (Promise)
"They will help you with the project." (Willingness)
In each of these cases, the action is in the future, and there is a sense of certainty or decisiveness about the occurrence of the event.

Future Continuous Tense

The future continuous tense, on the other hand, is used for actions that will be in progress at a specific point in the future. It often implies that the action will happen automatically, or it highlights the duration of the action rather than its completion. This tense is formed with "will be" followed by the present participle (the -ing form) of the verb.

Consider these examples:

"She will be traveling to France this time next year." (Emphasizes the action's duration)
"At noon, I will be finishing the report." (Focuses on the action taking place at a specific time)
"They will be helping you with the project all day tomorrow." (Highlights the ongoing nature of the help)
Here, the actions are not just set in the future; they are also expected to be happening at a particular future moment.

Distinguishing the Tenses in Practice

To better understand the difference, consider these contrasting examples:

Sample Exercises

Write five sentences using the simple future tense about plans for the upcoming holiday.

Solution:
"We will visit our grandparents in the countryside."
"She will buy gifts for her friends before Christmas."

Solution:
"She will be buying gifts for her friends on Christmas Eve."
"The city will be holding a parade when the clock strikes midnight on New Year's Eve."
"They will be announcing the New Year's resolutions during the end-of-year meeting."
"I will be making a special dinner for the family on Christmas night."
Creative Application

Imagine you are writing a short story set in the future. Your protagonist has a busy day ahead and their schedule is packed. Try using both tenses to convey not only what they will do but also what they will be doing at specific times during the day.

For example:

Simple Future: Tomorrow is the day of the great space race. Lyla will pilot her rocket at the break of dawn. She will meet her rival, Orion, on the asteroid belt by noon. Afterward, she will claim the trophy at the Galactic Council.

Future Continuous: While the stars still shimmer, Lyla will be piloting her craft, navigating through the silence of space.

By the time the sun reaches its zenith, she will be meeting Orion, with their ships shadow-dancing in the asteroid belt. And as the universe watches, she will be claiming her victory among a constellation of applause.

In Summary

The simple future is your go-to for promises, predictions, and decisions about the future, while the future continuous gives your sentences a texture, emphasizing the ongoing nature of future events. Both tenses offer richness to the language, allowing speakers to express subtleties about their intentions and the timing of future actions.

Understanding the future continuous tense is akin to setting your sights on a horizon where actions unfold in a rhythm that marches to the ticks of an imminent clock. This tense wraps around actions with a shroud of inevitability and continuity, an echo of the things that, while not yet started, have already taken a vivid shape in the realm of 'soon-to-be'.

Vivid Examples of the Future Continuous Tense
Foretelling with Precision: Suppose the hands of the clock are inching towards 10 AM today. You might paint a picture of tomorrow for your teammate, saying, "At the very stroke of 10 in the morrow, I shall be unveiling our strategic vision to the council."

Dental Appointments and Time's March: Envision the looming dental appointment you dread. Inform your spouse, "Come next Friday's afternoon, in the realm of three o'clock, I shall be ensconced in the dentist's stronghold, enduring the ritual of teeth-tending."

Actions Intertwined by Time: Ponder a Saturday laden with tasks and friendship. Declare your plans, "Whilst you shall be mastering the flames for our feast, I shall be adorning our haven with garlands and gleaming lights."

Forecasts amidst the Dawn: Take a weather forecaster's prophetic tone, "When tomorrow's dawn unfurls her rosy fingers, the sun shall be ascending its throne, bathing our world in hues of amber and fire."

The Dance of Routine: For the train that adheres to its schedule, you say, "As the clock chimes the sixth hour of the evening, the steel chariot shall be gracing the station's presence."

A Day's Flow Interrupted: If your day is a canvas of endless tasks, share with an inquiring friend, "I shall be deep in the embrace of work, from sunup till its retreat, yet for thee, I can carve out a moment."

Queries Cloaked in Courtesy: Should you seek to borrow the family car, ask gently, "Might I inquire if you shall be claiming the carriage's services come this eventide?"

Conjectures on Tomorrow: Suppose you are contemplating a friend's whereabouts, "He, entwined in his scholarly pursuits, shall be absent from our nightly revelries."

Creative Practice Exercises for the Future Continuous Tense
Exercise 1: Weaving Time with Your Words
Reflect on the mosaic of your typical weekday. Craft five sentences, each a thread leading to a different moment, all clothed in the future continuous tense.

Conjure the image of a friend's surprise festivity. Weave a narrative that captures the essence of what each conspirator shall be doing in preparation.

Exercise 2: Time Bending - Correct the Tense
Given are phrases in the simpler future's cloak. Transmute them into the future continuous tense, adding layers of depth and continuity.

I shall engage with a book upon your arrival.

They shall consume the evening meal when the clock strikes seven.

Next month, her journey shall take her to New York's embrace.

This weekend, the cinema shall capture our attention.

Tonight, his labors shall extend into the moon's watch.

Exercise 3: The Art of Polite Future Inquiries

Craft five inquiries, each a gentle probe into future endeavors, using the future continuous tense as your chisel and canvas in a professional gallery.

Exercise 4: A Tapestry of Tomorrow - Storytelling

Spin a tale where each thread is a future continuous strand, illustrating a character's tapestry of activities from the dawn's blush to the twilight's sigh.

Exercise 5: The Symphony of the Unexpected

Narrate a day's script in which the acts shall be pierced by an unforeseen interlude. Let the future continuous tense sing the melody of planned endeavors and sudden diversions.

Imaginative Solutions to the Practice Exercises

Solution to Exercise 1:

As tomorrow's first light breaks, I shall be engaging with the morning breeze on my way to the forge of my daily toils. Come the tenth toll of the day's bell, in the congregation of minds, I shall be presenting our collective musings. The sun at its zenith shall find me amidst camaraderie and sustenance. In the waning afternoon, collaboration shall be my ship, and creation my sea. And as the day wanes, I shall be cleaving through the park's embrace, the wind my silent companion.

Solution to Exercise 2:

I shall be delving into the book's realm when you make your presence known.

They shall be amidst the ritual of dining as the seventh hour manifests.

She shall be coursing through the skies towards New York as the new month unfolds.

We shall be lost in the film's unfolding tapestry this coming weekend.

He shall be laboring under the night's watchful gaze this eve.

Solution to Exercise 3:

Will you be stewarding the conference room's vessel on this afternoon's tide?

Could I inquire if assistance will be something you shall be desiring on the morrow's presentation?

Is the next week's workshop something you shall be gracing with your presence?

Might I seek knowledge on whether the Friday's client discourse shall have you at its helm?

Dare I ask if the project's chronicle shall be receiving your touch later this day?

Solution to Exercise 4:

In the nascent hours of the day, Emma shall be battling with the embrace of sleep as her alarm tolls its war-cry. As the city stirs, she shall be a silent observer, her tea's steam the only cloud in a clear sky. The sun's zenith shall be her stage, her ideas the actors in a play of progress. And as the day dons its evening shawl, she shall be basking in the glow of her triumph, the city's hum a distant chorus to the laughter around her.

Solution to Exercise 5:

On the forthcoming Tuesday, I shall be in the throes of creation, my painting an unborn rainbow on the canvas. The air shall be thick with the scent of potential and pigment. As the clock's hands unite in the afternoon, an interruption shall unfurl; a call shall arrive bearing tidings of victory in art's arena. The day's plans shall be upended as I shall be thrust into a whirlwind of preparation, the anticipation a wild stallion in my breast.

In practicing these exercises, one not only hones the ability to cloak future actions in the garb of continuity and expectancy but also embellishes one's linguistic wardrobe with the rich tapestries of the future continuous tense.

Chapter 10: The Future Perfect Tense

The future perfect tense is a verb form that we use to describe actions that will have been completed by a certain point in the future. The construction of the future perfect tense involves the auxiliary verb "will," followed by the auxiliary "have," and then the past participle of the main verb. This tense is particularly useful when projecting ourselves forward in time and looking back at an action that will be finished.

For instance, the future perfect sentence, "By 2025, she will have completed her studies," implies that at some point in time, when we reach the year 2025, the action of her completing her studies is something that will already be in the past. It is a tense that gives us the power to predict and place actions on a timeline that hasn't yet unfolded, but with certainty that they will have taken place by a certain moment.

Let's delve deeper and discover the layers of the future perfect tense's usage, the technicalities behind its construction, and some of the rare and practical applications it holds in both written and spoken English.

Understanding the Technical Structure
To form the future perfect tense, you follow this formula: will + have + past participle. The past participle is a form of the verb that typically, though not always, ends in -ed for regular verbs. For example:

"I will have walked ten miles by noon."
These sentences highlight an important characteristic of the future perfect: it tells us that not only will an action be completed, it also emphasizes the duration or the amount of time spent on the action.

Usage in Various Contexts
The future perfect is used in multiple contexts, which include but are not limited to:

Completion of Action by a Specific Time: As mentioned, this is the primary use of the future perfect tense, to state that an action will be finished before a certain future moment.

Duration up to a Point in the Future: It can also emphasize the length of time an action will have been happening once it's completed.

Cause and Effect Situations in the Future: Sometimes it's used to express the idea that something will have happened as a result of another future action.

Rare Knowledge about Future Perfect
One interesting aspect of the future perfect that is not widely taught is its implied sense of certainty. When you use the future perfect tense, you express a strong conviction that something will happen. There's a subtle nuance that what you're discussing is almost inevitable.

Moreover, native speakers often use the future perfect tense in a rhetorical way. For example, a parent might say to a child, "By the time you realize I'm right, you will have learned it the hard way." Here, the future perfect adds a tone of wisdom and foresight to the sentence.

Practical Applications
In real-world scenarios, the future perfect can be found in business settings, academic planning, event organizing, and even casual conversations about future aspirations or goals. For example, project managers often use this tense to assure stakeholders of a project's timeline: "By the third quarter, we will have launched the new platform."

128

Creative Style and Unique Usage
In storytelling, writers might use the future perfect tense for foreshadowing or to create suspense. It's a powerful tool to let readers know that certain events will transpire, without revealing how they come about.

Sample Exercises
To master the future perfect tense, consider the following exercises:

Complete the Sentence: Take a sentence fragment and finish it using the future perfect tense.

Fragment: "By the time you get this letter..."
True or False Predictions: Make a future perfect prediction about yourself or a fictional character, and later discuss whether it turned out to be true or false.

Analysis: (This would be done at the end of the year to check the truth of the prediction.)
Create a Timeline: List events in the future perfect tense that will happen at specific times in the future.

"By 6 AM, I will have woken up."
"By 9 AM, I will have arrived at work."
Incorporating the future perfect into daily language practice can solidify understanding. For language learners, it's often about getting comfortable with the construction and knowing when it's appropriate to use this tense.

To truly appreciate the future perfect tense, it's helpful to use it in a variety of sentences. It's a grammatical structure that requires a bit of thought but can add precision and clarity to your statements about the future. By using the future perfect tense, you can succinctly communicate outcomes and expectations, which is particularly valuable in professional and academic environments

The future perfect tense in English grammar is used to describe an action that will be completed by a certain point in the future. This tense offers a glimpse into the future, akin to looking at a snapshot of what will have been achieved as time marches on. Crafting sentences in the future perfect involves a combination of "will," "have," and the past participle of the main verb.

To build an affirmative sentence in the future perfect tense, you begin with the subject, follow with "will have," and conclude with the past participle of the verb. For example:

By the end of the decade, scientists will have discovered new sustainable energy sources.
In this sentence, we express a positive belief about what scientists will achieve by a specific time in the future. The structure is confident, casting a prediction that is both hopeful and steeped in the potential of human innovation.

Shifting to the negative form, the structure is only slightly altered, introducing "not" after "will." The negative form carries the weight of a prediction that is absent or unrealized. Consider this:

By the next century, humanity will not have found a way to live on Mars.
Here, the negative form signals a doubt or a limitation, suggesting that despite our aspirations, certain achievements may remain out of reach within the specified timeframe.

The interrogative form of the future perfect tense is used to ask questions about what will have occurred by a certain point in the future. It flips the structure, starting with "will," followed by the subject, "have," and the past participle. For example:

Will we have learned to coexist peacefully with artificial intelligence by 2050?
In this question, there's a sense of curiosity and contemplation. It seeks to explore our readiness to adapt and harmonize with the advancements that loom on the horizon.

Let's delve further into these structures with unique content and creative flair, weaving in technical knowledge and rare insights, along with practical applications. We will explore these in scenarios across different fields such as science, technology, and cultural development, capped with sample exercises to solidify our understanding.

Affirmative Future Perfect Tense
Imagine a future where the threads of current scientific exploration have woven into the fabric of reality. The affirmative future perfect tense shines a light on these possibilities.

Space Exploration: By 2040, astronauts will have established a permanent base on the moon, acting as a springboard for deeper space exploration.

In this sentence, the certainty with which we speak of the lunar base paints a picture of a determined and technologically advanced civilization, reaching for the stars quite literally.

Technology: By the end of this year, engineers will have completed the prototype of a quantum computer that can outperform traditional computers in complex calculations.

The sentence encapsulates the optimism in technological progress, suggesting a breakthrough that could revolutionize computing.

Medicine: By the next decade, doctors will have perfected the use of gene editing to cure genetic disorders, ushering in a new era of personalized medicine.

This forecasts a monumental stride in medical science, pointing to a future where diseases could be snipped away at their genetic roots.

Negative Future Perfect Tense
Negations in the future perfect tense often carry a poignant message of caution or a sobering reminder of our limitations.

Environmental Challenges: By 2050, we will not have halted the progression of climate change, but we will have learned vital lessons about balancing industrial growth with environmental stewardship.

The sentence strikes a chord of realism, suggesting that while progress is inevitable, it comes with the cost of hard-earned lessons.

Artificial Intelligence: By the end of the century, AI will not have replaced all human jobs, but it will have transformed the employment landscape significantly.

This reflects the nuanced understanding that technology reshapes, rather than completely overwrites, the tapestry of human labor.

Sociocultural Evolution: In fifty years, societies will not have resolved all cultural conflicts, but they will have made significant strides toward mutual respect and understanding.

Here, we touch upon the intricate journey of human coexistence, recognizing both our aspirations and the complex nature of cultural dynamics.

Interrogative Future Perfect Tense
The interrogative form serves as a beacon, casting questions into the future, prompting us to envision what lies ahead.

Space Travel: Will humans have set foot on Mars by 2035?

This question stirs the imagination, inviting us to consider the timeline and ambition of our extraterrestrial endeavors.

Technological Integration: Will we have integrated augmented reality into daily life to the extent that it becomes indistinguishable from physical reality?

Here, the question probes the extent of technological convergence with our perception of reality, questioning the implications of such an evolution.

Cultural Heritage: Will we have preserved the diverse languages currently at risk of extinction in our increasingly globalized world?

This seeks to understand our commitment to cultural preservation in the face of homogenizing forces.

Sample Exercises
Now, let's construct exercises to apply these concepts in practice.

Exercise 1: Create an Affirmative Sentence
Imagine a technological advancement that interests you. Predict its completion using the future perfect tense.

Example Answer: By 2025, researchers will have unveiled an AI system that can predict natural disasters with high accuracy, potentially saving countless lives.

Exercise 2: Form a Negative Sentence
Consider an environmental challenge. Express a realistic limitation using the future perfect negative form.

Example Answer: Despite our efforts, by 2040, we will not have stopped the loss of biodiversity in the rainforests.

Exercise 3: Ask an Interrogative Sentence
Think of a social issue. Ask a question about its future resolution using the future perfect tense.

Example Answer: Will society have found a balance between privacy and security in the era of digital surveillance by 2030?

Engaging with these exercises encourages us to think critically about the future, employing the future perfect tense as both a grammatical tool and a lens through which to consider what lies ahead.

The future perfect tense is a verb form that describes actions that will have been completed by a certain point in the future. It is useful for expressing expectations, predictions, or assumptions about situations in the future, particularly in relation to a specific time.

To understand the practical applications of the future perfect tense, let's consider a few scenarios:

Project Completion:
Imagine you are a project manager, and you have a deadline to meet. You might say, "By the end of this quarter, we will have completed the initial phase of the construction." This implies that when the quarter ends, the action of completing the initial phase will be finished.

Life Milestones:
A person thinking about life goals might say, "By the time I turn 30, I will have traveled to at least ten countries." This reflects an expectation or an aspiration about personal achievements that the person assumes will be accomplished before turning 30.

Academic Achievements:
A student might state, "By the end of this academic year, I will have mastered the basics of quantum mechanics." This shows the student's confidence and assumption that the learning goals will be met before the specified time.

Professional Growth:
In a professional setting, an employee might predict, "By next year, I will have gained the necessary skills to be considered for a promotion." This sentence suggests that there is an ongoing process of skill acquisition that is expected to be complete by the stipulated time frame.

Personal Projects:
For personal endeavors, one might plan, "By September, I will have finished writing my novel." This reflects a clear goal and the timeframe within which the person expects to achieve it.

Now, let's create a few sample exercises to demonstrate the use of the future perfect tense:

Exercise 1:
Complete the sentences with the future perfect tense:

By 10 AM, I _____ (finish) my report.
She _____ (make) all the necessary arrangements by the time the guests arrive.
We _____ (learn) all the topics in the syllabus before the semester ends.
Solutions:

By 10 AM, I will have finished my report.
She will have made all the necessary arrangements by the time the guests arrive.
We will have learned all the topics in the syllabus before the semester ends.
Exercise 2:
Rewrite the sentences in the future perfect tense:

I finish my thesis. (by next month)
They plant a garden. (by the end of spring)
You read the entire book. (before the book club meeting)

Solutions:

By the end of spring, they will have planted a garden.
Before the book club meeting, you will have read the entire book.

Exercise 3:
Write three sentences using the future perfect tense to describe what you will have achieved by a certain age.

Sample Sentences:

By the age of 35, I will have established my own business.
By the age of 50, I will have visited all seven continents.
By the age of 40, I will have written at least three novels.
Understanding the future perfect tense is particularly useful in many professional contexts, where precise communication about project timelines and goals is crucial. It allows individuals to set clear expectations and convey confidence about future outcomes. This tense is not just about expressing certainty; it also subtly communicates the effort and planning involved in achieving future goals. It can be motivational, prompting both speakers and listeners to consider the steps required to accomplish their objectives within a given timeframe.

Creatively, the future perfect can add depth to writing, particularly in storytelling where the author might foreshadow future events, or in character development, to show ambitions and plans. It can convey a sense of destiny or fate, a path set out before the characters that they are moving towards inexorably.

In summary, the future perfect tense serves as a powerful tool in language to express completed actions in a future context, implying a sense of vision, accomplishment, and foresight. Its mastery is essential for effective communication in both everyday life and professional settings, enhancing the clarity and depth of our conversations about the future.

Delving into the rich tapestry of English tenses, the future perfect is akin to a masterful stroke of a painter, ensuring that the picture of our intentions in time is both complete and finely detailed by a specific moment yet to come. In stark contrast, the various other tenses of future action act as broad brushes, coloring our intentions with different shades of certainty, planning, and spontaneity.

The Tapestry of Future Tense

Future Perfect vs. Future Simple

Where the future simple is the quick sketch of what's to come, formed with the trusty "will" or "shall" followed by the verb's simplest form, it's the spontaneous promise or the casual forecast, unfettered by the constraints of exact times.

Future Simple Sketch: "I shall pen a report." (A mere intention to write a report, with no clock ticking in the background.)
Future Perfect Masterstroke: "By the time Friday unfurls its calendar page, my report shall be a completed chapter." (Here lies precision; the report isn't just an intention—it's an impending fact, framed by Friday's deadline.)
Future Perfect vs. Present Continuous for Future

Present continuous for future actions is the artist's outline of plans, a pencil tracing of events that have a place and time already decided.

Present Continuous Outline: "I am slated to confer with the team on the morrow." (It's etched in schedules; the meeting is as certain as sunrise.)
Future Perfect Completion: "Come the morrow, my consultation with the team shall be but a memory." (This

gives a sense of an event that, by the specified future time, will be etched in the past.)
Future Perfect vs. Future Continuous

The future continuous paints a scene of activity, a segment of time wherein actions will be unfolding, alive and in motion.

Future Continuous Brushstroke: "When afternoon shadows grow tomorrow, I shall be in the midst of report-crafting." (An action captured mid-movement, the subject enwrapped in their task.)
Future Perfect Finishing Touch: "As twilight calls tomorrow, the narrative of my report will have its ending writ." (The action is no longer a process—it's a deed done, the end of the tale.)
Future Perfect vs. "Going to" Future

"Going to" is the painter's intention, a plan that's expected to manifest based on the present landscape or as an expression of determined action.

"Going to" Draft: "I am poised to compose a report, the survey results as my muse." (The intent is clear, and the muse is present, the plan ready to be set in motion.)
Future Perfect Portrait: "When the new week dawns, the survey will have spoken through the prose of my report." (A vision of the future where the plan has become a completed act.)
Practical Applications in Life's Canvas

Grasping these tenses' nuances empowers eloquence in our daily interactions, particularly where the clarity of timeframes is non-negotiable. Imagine a project conductor, weaving assurance into conversations with the future perfect, or a collaborator, painting their upcoming endeavors in the continuous hues of the future tense.

Exercises to Sculpt Your Tense Mastery

Let us breathe life into these concepts with practical exercises:

1. Tense Transformation Challenge:

Sculpt in Future Simple: "Our collective will usher forth the website anew in June."
Re-sculpted in Future Perfect: "When June's warmth graces us, the website will stand renewed, our collective's efforts realized."
In crafting singular and specialized content, we find that the future perfect tense, though perhaps less frequented than its temporal kin, offers a unique vessel to convey certainty and the completed state of future endeavors. Its mastery is not only an asset but a beacon of precision in the seas of English communication, especially valuable for those navigating the waters of technical or detail-focused vocations.

The future perfect tense in English is used to describe actions that will have been completed by a certain point in the future. It gives a sense of completion and is formed by using "will have" followed by the past participle of the main verb.

Here's a comprehensive exploration of the future perfect tense, including examples and exercises.

Understanding the Future Perfect Tense:

Imagine you're planning a garden. You predict that by next spring, you will have planted many flowers. You're looking ahead to a specific time and anticipating an action will be finished by that point.

The future perfect can also indicate a duration of time before a certain point in the future. If you say, "By 2025, I will have worked here for 10 years," you're stating that when 2025 arrives, the action of working will have reached its ten-year mark.

Usage of Future Perfect Tense:

Completion of an action by a certain future time: "They will have completed the project by next month."

Examples in Different Contexts:
Daily Life: By the time we get to the party, the host will have prepared all the food.
Education: By the end of this semester, the students will have read all the required books.
Professional Setting: The company will have launched the new product before the trade show begins.
Personal Goals: I will have run a marathon before I turn 30.
Exercises for Practice:

Completion Exercise:
By the time you call me tonight, I _____ (finish) my homework.
She _____ (not/eat) by the time we arrive, so we can all dine together.
They _____ (move) into their new home by next week.
Solutions:

By the time you call me tonight, I will have finished my homework.
She will not have eaten by the time we arrive, so we can all dine together.
They will have moved into their new home by next week.
Error Correction:

By the end of the day, he will finishes his work. (Correct: he will have finished)
I will have learned French before I move to Paris next year. (Correct: No error)

We will have understand the lesson before we have to apply it. (Correct: understood)
Multiple Choice:

By 2025, I _____ (will finish / will have finished / finish) studying at the university.
They _____ (will have built / builds / will build) the bridge by the end of next year.
She _____ (will have been / will be / is) teaching there for a decade by the time you graduate.
Solutions:

By 2025, I will have finished studying at the university.
They will have built the bridge by the end of next year.
She will have been teaching there for a decade by the time you graduate.
Creative Application:

Let's apply the future perfect tense in a short narrative to see how it helps in storytelling.

Future Perfect Story: The Time Capsule

In the heart of the town, under the ancient oak tree, the townspeople will have gathered on New Year's Eve, 2050. They will have come together to unearth a time capsule buried 50 years ago. The mayor will have prepared a speech, and the children will have rehearsed a play. As the clock will have struck midnight, and the capsule is opened, each person will have shared a piece of history. By the end of the night, stories that will have been locked away for decades will once again fill the air, connecting generations.

Write Your Own Story:

Create a short story using the future perfect tense. Imagine a significant event in the future and describe the actions that will have been completed by that time. For example, consider a family preparing for a reunion, a team working towards a major project deadline, or a couple planning a milestone anniversary celebration.

Remember to use a variety of sentence structures and to incorporate both the completion of actions and the duration aspect of the future perfect tense.

Chapter 11: The Present Perfect Continuous Tense

The present perfect continuous tense in English is used to describe an action that began in the past and continues up to the present, often with a focus on the duration of the action. It is formed using the present perfect tense of the verb "to be" (have/has been) followed by the present participle (the -ing form) of the main verb.

For instance, consider the sentence: "She has been reading for three hours." Here, 'has been reading' is the present perfect continuous tense, indicating that she started reading in the past and is still reading now. The emphasis is on the process of reading and the time spent doing it.

Let's delve deeper into its usage with various examples and exercises.

Usage of Present Perfect Continuous Tense
The present perfect continuous can be used in several scenarios:

Duration of an Ongoing Action: When we want to express the duration of an action that started in the past and is still happening.

Temporary Actions and Situations: It can describe temporary actions or situations that may not be finished at the moment of speaking. "He has been staying with us while his house is being repaired."

Actions Repeated Over a Period of Time: To talk about actions that have occurred repeatedly over a period up until now. "She has been practicing piano every day for her recital."

Cause of a Present Situation: When explaining the cause of a present situation. "Why are you sweating? - I have been running."

Emphasis on the Action's Duration: Whenever there's a need to emphasize how long an action has been taking place, rather than the action itself. "They have been negotiating the contract for months."

Exercises to Understand Present Perfect Continuous Tense
Let's now create some sample exercises and solve them to understand the concept better:

Exercise 1: Identifying Present Perfect Continuous Tense
Read the following sentences and identify if they are written in the present perfect continuous tense:

The children are playing in the garden.
They will be joining us for dinner later.
He has been learning French for two years.
We have lived in this city for a decade.
Solution:

Sentences 2 and 4 are in the present perfect continuous tense.

Exercise 2: Forming Sentences Using Present Perfect Continuous Tense
Form sentences using the present perfect continuous tense from the following cues:

(write / an essay / for three hours)
(watch / television / since 7 PM)
(work / on the project / all week)
Solution:

"I have been writing an essay for three hours."
"They have been watching television since 7 PM."
"We have been working on the project all week."

Exercise 3: Transforming Sentences
Transform the following sentences into present perfect continuous tense:

The birds fly south every winter.
She reads a book.
I am studying for the test.
Solution:

The present perfect continuous tense is not applicable because the action is habitual, not ongoing. However, if we imagine an ongoing situation, it might be: "The birds have been flying south since the winter began."
To transform this into present perfect continuous: "She has been reading a book for some time now."
Exercise 4: Combining Sentences Using Present Perfect Continuous Tense
Combine the following pairs of sentences using the present perfect continuous tense:

He started to play the guitar. It was five years ago.
They began their journey. It was early morning.
Solution:

"They have been traveling since early morning."
Practical Applications
In practical terms, the present perfect continuous tense serves to bridge the past with the present. It is especially helpful in conversational English to describe experiences, explain current states of being that are linked to past actions, and to highlight the duration of activities in progress.

In professional settings, this tense might be used to describe ongoing projects ("We have been developing the new software for six months."), in customer service to address ongoing issues ("We have been addressing the outage since it was first reported."), or to convey persistent efforts ("The team has been working tirelessly to meet the deadline.").

Understanding and using the present perfect continuous tense effectively can greatly enhance your fluency in English and allow you to convey messages with the desired emphasis on the continuity and duration of actions. It's a vital aspect of conveying the sense of an ongoing process or activity in relation to the present moment, thus enriching communication with temporal depth and specificity.

Understanding the Present Perfect Continuous tense in English requires recognizing that it denotes an action that began in the past and continues up to the present moment, often with effects or implications for the current situation. This tense is formed with the auxiliary verbs "have" or "has," depending on the subject, followed by "been" and the present participle (the -ing form) of the main verb.

The structure for affirmative sentences is as follows: Subject + has/have + been + present participle of the verb (+ object/complement).

Let's explore this through various contexts and examples.

Affirmative Sentences in the Present Perfect Continuous Tense

A scientist working on a lengthy experiment might say, "I have been studying these bacterial cultures for over two months."
An athlete training for a competition may reflect, "I have been training every day to improve my stamina."
A student immersed in their studies could state, "I have been learning French for the past year."
A writer engaged in crafting a novel might comment, "I have been writing my book since January."
An environmentalist could observe, "We have been tracking the migratory patterns of these birds for several seasons."
These sentences affirm that an action started in the past and continues at the moment of speaking. The speaker is often

emphasizing the duration of the activity and its ongoing nature.

Negative Sentences in the Present Perfect Continuous Tense

For the negative form, we simply insert "not" between "have/has" and "been":

Subject + has/have + not + been + present participle of the verb (+ object/complement).

Here are some inventive examples in negative forms:

A musician taking a break might say, "I have not been practicing my guitar regularly this month."
A traveler who has paused their journey could state, "I have not been exploring new countries since the outbreak began."
A gardener during winter may lament, "I have not been tending to my garden since the frost set in."
A researcher who has hit a roadblock might admit, "I have not been making significant progress in my experiments lately."
A teacher on summer vacation could reflect, "I have not been teaching since the school year ended."
In these sentences, the negative form indicates that the expected continuous action has not been happening up to the present or has been interrupted.

Interrogative Sentences in the Present Perfect Continuous Tense

To form interrogative sentences, we invert the subject and "have/has":

Have/Has + subject + been + present participle of the verb (+ object/complement)?

Consider these questions as they might arise in different scenarios:

A project manager inquiring about a task might ask, "Have you been working on the report all afternoon?"
A fitness coach questioning an athlete could inquire, "Has she been following her training schedule diligently?"
A curious colleague might probe, "Have we been focusing too much on one aspect of the project?"
A nutritionist consulting a client could question, "Have you been maintaining the dietary changes we discussed?"
A teacher evaluating a student's progress might ask, "Has he been practicing his reading skills regularly?"
These questions are used to seek information about the duration and continuity of actions up to the present moment.

Sample Exercise:

Let's solidify our understanding with an exercise. Convert the following sentences from affirmative to negative and interrogative forms:

"She has been organizing the annual conference since March."
"They have been contributing to the community fund for a decade."

Using the Present Perfect Continuous tense effectively allows you to describe ongoing actions with a certain depth and specificity that other tenses cannot provide. It places the focus not just on the action itself, but on its duration and relevance to the present moment. Whether in writing or speech, mastering this tense can add precision and clarity to your communication.

The present perfect continuous tense serves as a linguistic bridge, connecting past actions to their present state or influence. It is crafted by combining the present perfect form of the verb 'to be'—'have' or 'has been'—with the main verb's 'ing' form, giving life to sentences that breathe with continuity and duration.

Imagine we are discussing the educational journey of someone: "For a trio of years, she has immersed herself in the English language." The essence here is that the journey of learning did not reach its terminus three years ago; instead, it persists, actively unwinding even as we speak.

Let's cast our nets wider and explore the various facets of the present perfect continuous tense, including its structure and real-world applications. Additionally, I will craft exercises to solidify your grasp of this tense.

Structuring the Present Perfect Continuous Tense

The architecture of this tense is a dance of words where 'have/has been' twirls around the main verb adorned with an 'ing', depicting actions unfurling over time.

The Elapsed Time and Ongoing Actions

Commonly, we deploy this tense to underline the stretch of time across which an action extends. Phrases like "for two hours" or "since last winter" serve as temporal markers, anchoring our sense of duration.

For example:

"Upon this endeavor, we have been laboring for a quintet of months."
Echoes of Recent Endeavors

Moreover, this tense can cast light on recent undertakings with lingering present effects. For example, if one declares, "I've engaged in the culinary arts," the implication might be of an action either freshly completed or still in progress, hinted by the aroma in the air or the feast laid out.

For instance:

"The soil clings to her apparel; she has been tending to her garden."
Real-World Implications

In the realm of professionalism, this tense often surfaces in dialogues about ongoing projects or to detail periods of occupational engagement.

For instance:

"I've been engaging with the ivories of the piano, and delightfully, the journey prospers."
Artistic Exploits

Artists and scribes may employ the present perfect continuous with a flair for the dramatic, infusing a sense of the eternal into their narratives.

Ponder this literary expression:

"For aeons, the venerable oak has stood sentinel, its boughs bearing witness to the village's whispered legends."
Exercises for Mastery

Let's conceive some scenarios to practice molding sentences in the present perfect continuous tense.

Meld the following using the present perfect continuous tense:

"Jane engages in the art of painting. Her start was two hours prior."
Solution: "For two hours, Jane has been engaged in the artistry of painting."
Complete the sentence by injecting the present perfect continuous form of the verb:

"Fatigue is etched upon your visage. Have you _____ (to work) since twilight?"
Solution: "Fatigue is etched upon your visage. Have you been toiling since twilight?"
From the provided terms, fabricate a sentence in the present perfect continuous tense:

Solution: "Mark has been engaged with the same narrative since the previous month."
Transform the following into the present perfect continuous tense:

"The visionaries probe into novel sustainable energies. Their quest commenced five years past."
Form a question in the present perfect continuous tense using the given words:

"Have they been engaged in the crafting of the new cyber construct?"
Regular engagement with such exercises can hone your command over the present perfect continuous tense. It's a craft of not only constructing sentences accurately but also weaving the temporal fabric of when and why this tense should illuminate your dialogues. Its mastery affords a communicator the ability to paint actions with the brush of time, offering narratives that are textured with duration and continuity.

    The distinction between the present perfect continuous tense and the present perfect tense is subtle yet important, reflecting different aspects of time and action in the English language. Both tenses link past actions to the present moment but emphasize different elements of the action or state.

Present Perfect Continuous Tense
This tense is utilized to describe an action that began in the past and is still continuing in the present or has recently

stopped, with emphasis on the continuity or duration of the action. The structure involves the present tense of the auxiliary verb 'to have' (have/has), the past participle 'been,' and the present participle (the '-ing' form) of the main verb.

Examples:

I have been reading a book on quantum mechanics. (The action of reading may still be ongoing or has just finished, but the effect of it, perhaps knowledge or enjoyment, is relevant now.)
She has been working at the laboratory for five years.
Present Perfect Tense
In contrast, the present perfect tense is employed to indicate an action that happened at an unspecified time in the past. The focus is on the result of the action rather than the duration or process. It uses the present tense of 'to have' along with the past participle of the main verb.

Examples:

I have read a book on quantum mechanics. (This implies that the action is complete. The time when it was read is not specified; the importance is that it's done.)
She has worked on three groundbreaking experiments. (The statement summarizes completed actions without focusing on the continuity of working on them.)
Distinctive Applications
Emphasis on Duration vs. Completion
The present perfect continuous places the emphasis on the activity's duration: "I have been studying for hours." It suggests that the studying may still be happening or has very recently stopped. On the other hand, the present perfect suggests completion and is often used when the result of the activity is in focus: "I have studied enough for today," which suggests the studying is completed for now.

Temporary vs. Permanent Situations
We often use the present perfect continuous for temporary actions or situations: "They have been living in Paris for a month." Conversely, the present perfect may suggest a more permanent state

Repeated Actions
The present perfect can be used to indicate an action that has been repeated multiple times in the past: "We have visited that museum several times." The continuous form is less common in this context, but when used, it can suggest repetition that is unusually frequent: "She has been visiting that museum every day this week."

Cause of Present Situation
The present perfect continuous can often explain the cause of a present situation: "He is tired because he has been running." The present perfect might just state a fact about the past with a present consequence: "He has run five marathons."

Time Expressions
Certain time expressions are commonly used with these tenses. For instance, "for" and "since" can be used with both, but you'll find "recently" or "lately" more with the continuous to indicate a recent, ongoing action: "I have been feeling great lately."

Creative Illustration Through Sample Exercises
Let's imagine we're exploring the field of astrophotography.

Exercise 1: Describe an ongoing study about a celestial event.

Sample Answer:
I have been observing the trajectory of the comet since its discovery. This consistent observation allows us to gather long-term data on its path and predict its future position in the sky.

Exercise 2: Summarize the findings of a completed study about a celestial event.

Sample Answer:
I have analyzed the data from the recent meteor shower. The analysis has led to a comprehensive understanding of its origin and provided insights into the solar system's dynamics.

Through exercises like these, we can better understand the practical applications of these tenses and how they shape our understanding of events in a temporal context.

In Conclusion
The choice between these two tenses is not just a matter of grammatical correctness but also of what the speaker intends to convey. The present perfect continuous can project an image of someone with their sleeves rolled up, in the midst of action, whereas the present perfect might show someone with their hands washed, looking back at a job done. It's about motion versus rest, process versus result, and engagement versus summary.

Understanding these subtleties allows for effective communication, especially in fields where precision of expression is paramount, such as scientific reporting, technical analysis, and research. Using the correct tense not only conveys the facts but also the context and the nuance behind them, thus enriching the narrative, whether it's about everyday life or complex concepts.

Using the present perfect continuous tense in English allows you to express actions that began in the past and are still continuing at the present moment, or have recently stopped but have an effect on the present. It's formed with the subject plus 'have/has been' and the '-ing' form of the verb.

Here's a guide with examples and exercises to practice the present perfect continuous tense, aiming to enhance your understanding and application of this aspect of English grammar.

1. Forming the Present Perfect Continuous Tense

The structure for this tense is:

Subject + has/have + been + present participle (verb+ing)
For example:

I have been reading.
She has been working.
2. Use Cases

The present perfect continuous tense is used to express:

Actions that started in the past and are still happening: "They have been waiting for two hours."
Actions that have recently stopped but have a result in the present: "He's tired because he has been jogging."
To show that something has been happening repeatedly over a period of time: "I have been practicing the piano every day for a month."
3. Examples

Now, let's look at some examples before we move to the exercises:

"I have been studying English for three years."
"It has been raining all day."
"They have been traveling since last summer, visiting various countries."
"We have been experiencing some problems with our computer network recently."

4. Exercises

Here are some exercises to practice forming and using the present perfect continuous tense. The answers will follow each exercise for you to check your understanding.

Exercise 1: Fill in the blanks using the present perfect continuous tense.

a. I _____ (work) on this project since January.
b. She _____ (learn) French for two years.
c. The children _____ (play) outside since morning.
d. It _____ (snow) since early morning.
e. We _____ (look) forward to our holiday for months.

Answers:

a. I have been working on this project since January.
b. She has been learning French for two years.
c. The children have been playing outside since morning.
d. It has been snowing since early morning.
e. We have been looking forward to our holiday for months.

Exercise 2: Correct the errors in the following sentences.

a. She has been wait for the doctor for over an hour.
b. We has been studying for the final exams all week.
c. It have been raining for three days straight.
d. They has been running a marathon when it started to hail.

Answers:

a. She has been waiting for the doctor for over an hour.
b. We have been studying for the final exams all week.
c. It has been raining for three days straight.
d. They have been running a marathon when it started to hail.

Exercise 3: Transform the sentences into negative form.

a. I have been feeling quite well lately.
b. The scientists have been researching the cause of the phenomenon for years.
c. He has been teaching at the university since 1998.
d. The company has been expanding its operations globally.

Answers:

a. I have not been feeling quite well lately.
b. The scientists have not been researching the cause of the phenomenon for years.
c. He has not been teaching at the university since 1998.
d. The company has not been expanding its operations globally.

Exercise 4: Ask questions using the present perfect continuous tense based on the statements given.

a. (She / to work / on her thesis)
b. (They / to play / football)
c. (He / to fix / the car)
d. (You / to watch / this TV series)

Answers:

a. Has she been working on her thesis?
b. Have they been playing football?
c. Has he been fixing the car?
d. Have you been watching this TV series?

Exercise 5: Create sentences using the present perfect continuous tense with the words provided.

a. I / to read / this book
b. You / to listen / to music
c. She / to travel / around Asia
d. We / to look for / a new house

e. They / to study / for their exams

Answers:

a. I have been reading this book.
b. You have been listening to music.
c. She has been traveling around Asia.
d. We have been looking for a new house.
e. They have been studying for their exams.

By working through these exercises, you practice not only the formation of the present perfect continuous tense but also its application in various contexts. It's essential to combine such exercises with real-life usage, like describing ongoing activities or situations that have occurred over a period up to the present moment. Keep practicing, and you will find that your grasp of this tense becomes more natural and intuitive.

Chapter 12: The Past Perfect Continuous Tense

The past perfect continuous tense, a fascinating and intricate aspect of the English language, is utilized to express an action that was ongoing before another action in the past. This tense adds depth and texture to our understanding of temporal relationships in narrative and discourse. To grasp its essence, we delve into its definition, structure, usage, and nuances over a detailed exploration.

Definition
The past perfect continuous tense, also known as the past perfect progressive tense, describes an action that started in the past and continued up to another point in the past. This tense is particularly useful in illustrating the duration or continuity of a past action before another past action or time.

Structure
The construction of the past perfect continuous tense involves a combination of the past perfect of the verb 'to be' (had been) and the present participle (verb+ing). The formula is:

Subject + had been + present participle (verb+ing) + objects/time reference

Usage
Duration Before Something in the Past: This tense often highlights the duration of an action leading up to a certain point in the past. For instance, "She had been waiting for three hours when he finally arrived." This sentence emphasizes the length of time she spent waiting.

Cause of Something in the Past: It is used to express the cause of a past situation. For example, "He was tired because he had been jogging."

Two Past Actions: When dealing with two actions in the past, it expresses the first action which had been ongoing before the second one.

Nuances and Advanced Usage

Interrupted Actions: This tense is often used to describe an action that was ongoing in the past and was interrupted by another action. E.g., "I had been reading when the lights went out."

Duration and Emphasis: It adds emphasis on the duration or process of the past action, not just the fact that it happened.

With 'Since' and 'For': Often used with time expressions like 'since' and 'for' to specify the duration. E.g., "She had been working there for five years when she got the promotion."

Past Repetition and Habit: It can describe an action that was a habit in the past. "He had been visiting that café every day before it closed down."

Common Mistakes

Confusing with Past Continuous: Unlike past continuous, which is used for actions ongoing at a specific past time, past perfect continuous emphasizes the duration before another past event.

Overuse: It's not necessary to use past perfect continuous if the duration isn't important. Sometimes, past simple or past perfect is more appropriate.

Incorrect Time References: Using incorrect time references like 'now' can lead to confusion, as this tense is strictly for past actions.

Practice Exercises

Creating Sentences: Write five sentences using the past perfect continuous tense to describe actions with clear duration before another past event.

Identifying Errors: Identify and correct the errors in these sentences:
"They were tired because they had been work all night."
Conclusion
The past perfect continuous tense is a powerful tool in the English language, providing a window into the duration and continuity of past actions. Its correct usage enhances narrative depth, bringing clarity and richness to temporal relationships in past events. Understanding and mastering this tense involves not only knowing its structure and basic usage but also appreciating its nuances and avoiding common pitfalls. Through practice and attention to detail, one can effectively utilize the past perfect continuous tense to convey complex temporal dynamics in English communication.

By integrating these insights into your linguistic toolkit, you enhance your ability to express temporal nuances in English, elevating both your spoken and written narratives to new levels of sophistication.

The past perfect continuous tense, a significant aspect of English grammar, plays a crucial role in conveying actions that were ongoing in the past before another past action interrupted them. This tense structure is vital for expressing duration and continuity of past actions up to a certain point in time. In this extensive exploration, we'll delve into the formation of affirmative, negative, and interrogative sentences in the past perfect continuous tense, accompanied by practical examples and exercises to enhance understanding.

1. Understanding the Past Perfect Continuous Tense
Definition and Usage:
The past perfect continuous tense, often used to stress the duration of an action that was in progress before another action in the past, combines aspects of the past perfect and the present continuous tenses. It typically includes a time reference, emphasizing the duration of the action.

Structure:

Affirmative: Subject + had been + present participle (verb+ing)
Negative: Subject + had not been + present participle
Interrogative: Had + subject + been + present participle?

2. Formation of Affirmative Sentences

Concept and Structure:

Affirmative sentences in the past perfect continuous tense assert that an action was happening over a period of time in the past. The formula is straightforward: the subject is followed by 'had been' and the present participle form of the verb.

Examples:

She had been reading for hours when I called.
They had been traveling for three days before reaching their destination.

3. Formation of Negative Sentences

Concept and Structure:

Negative sentences in this tense express that an action was not happening during a specified duration in the past. The structure involves adding 'not' between 'had' and 'been.'

Examples:

The team had not been performing well before the new coach arrived.

4. Formation of Interrogative Sentences

Concept and Structure:

Interrogative sentences in the past perfect continuous tense are formed by placing 'had' at the beginning of the sentence, followed by the subject and 'been.'

Examples:

Had you been working on the project long before it was canceled?

Had they been living here for years when you met them?

5. Practical Applications and Unique Insights

In Literature: Authors often use this tense to provide a backdrop for events or to build suspense.

In Everyday Conversation: It's useful for sharing experiences or inquiring about events in the past.

In Academic and Professional Settings: This tense can be used to present historical analyses or describe prolonged past actions in reports.

6. Exercises

Exercise 1: Convert the following sentences into the past perfect continuous tense.

They are working on the project. (Affirmative)
She is not studying for the exam. (Negative)
Are you waiting for someone? (Interrogative)

Exercise 2: Identify the errors in the following sentences and correct them.

He had been not sleeping well since last week.
Had she been understood the instructions before she started?
They had been working here since five years.

7. Solutions to Exercises

Solution to Exercise 1:

They had been working on the project.
She had not been studying for the exam.
Had you been waiting for someone?

Solution to Exercise 2:

Corrected: He had not been sleeping well since last week.
Corrected: Had she been understanding the instructions before she started?
Corrected: They had been working here for five years.

8. Conclusion

The past perfect continuous tense is a powerful grammatical tool, enabling detailed and nuanced expression of past actions and their duration. Its proper use enhances clarity in communication, particularly when discussing events with a significant time element in the past. Mastery of this tense, therefore, not only improves grammatical precision but also enriches one's ability to convey complex temporal relationships in English.

The past perfect continuous tense, a nuanced and intricate aspect of English grammar, is primarily employed to articulate actions that began in the past and persisted up until another specific point in the past. This tense is particularly effective in conveying the duration of actions and elucidating cause-and-effect relationships. In this exploration, we will delve into its usage, nuances, and practical applications, presenting unique content with a blend of technical knowledge and creativity.

1. Fundamental Understanding of Past Perfect Continuous Tense

The past perfect continuous tense, structured as "had been [present participle]," serves to emphasize the ongoing nature of past actions or events that were in progress before another past event intervened. It often includes a temporal element to specify the duration of the activity.

Example Exercise:
2. Duration of Actions
One of the primary uses of this tense is to highlight the duration of an action that continued over a period of time in the past.

Example Exercise:
Sentence: "They had been traveling around Europe for six months before they decided to settle in Italy."
Analysis: The duration of their travel (six months) is emphasized, leading up to their decision to settle.
3. Cause-and-Effect Relationships
The past perfect continuous can be instrumental in illustrating cause-and-effect relationships, especially in scenarios where the 'cause' is an ongoing action that leads to a specific 'effect'.

Example Exercise:
4. Emphasizing the Continuity of Past Actions
This tense also serves to stress the continuity or repetitiveness of a past action, often in a narrative context.

Example Exercise:
Sentence: "By the time she finished her thesis, she had been researching the topic for over four years."
Analysis: The sentence underscores the continuous effort and time spent on research.
5. Contrasting with Past Simple
Contrasting actions in the past perfect continuous with those in the past simple can highlight the difference between ongoing actions and specific, completed actions.

Example Exercise:
6. Using Time Expressions
Time expressions such as "for," "since," and "by the time" are commonly used with this tense to denote the duration and timing of actions.

Example Exercise:
Sentence: "They had been working on the project since January, and by June, they were ready to present it."
Analysis: This sentence uses time expressions to mark the start, duration, and endpoint of the action.
7. Specifying Reasons with Past Perfect Continuous
The tense is often used to specify the reasons behind a particular state or event in the past.

Example Exercise:
8. Complex Sentences Structure
Complex sentence structures using the past perfect continuous can add depth and clarity to narrative and descriptive writing.

Example Exercise:
9. Interplay with Other Tenses

Understanding how the past perfect continuous interacts with other tenses, like the past perfect simple or present perfect, can enhance clarity in storytelling and description.

Example Exercise:
10. Subtle Nuances and Advanced Usage
In literature and advanced narratives, the past perfect continuous can be used to convey subtle nuances of time, mood, and causality, enriching the storytelling experience.

Example Exercise:
Sentence: "Lost in her thoughts, she hadn't realized how long she had been walking along the shore."
Analysis: This sentence subtly conveys the duration and introspective nature of the walk.
Conclusion
The past perfect continuous tense is a sophisticated tool in the English language, enabling speakers and writers to convey duration, continuity, and causality of past actions with precision and depth. Its proper use can significantly enhance the expressiveness and clarity of communication, particularly in narrative and descriptive contexts.

Delving into the realm of English grammar, we find two fascinating aspects of past tense storytelling: the Past Perfect and Past Perfect Continuous tenses. These tenses are not mere grammatical constructs but tools that paint pictures of time and action in our linguistic canvas. Let's embark on an exploratory journey to understand and differentiate these two tenses, each rich in its narrative potential.

1. Laying the Groundwork: Grasping the Tenses
Past Perfect Tense: The Storyteller of Completed Actions
Imagine a scene frozen in time, where an action has already played out before another past moment. This is the essence of the Past Perfect tense, crafted by coupling 'had' with a verb's past participle.

For Instance:

Picture a meeting commencing, but before this moment, a manager had already crafted a report. This completion is the essence of Past Perfect.

Envision a student, homework done, now free to embrace the joy of play. Here again, the Past Perfect encapsulates a completed task.

Past Perfect Continuous Tense: The Narrator of Ongoing Past Journeys

In contrast, the Past Perfect Continuous paints a picture of an action in motion, a journey through time, culminating before another past event. It's woven with 'had been' and the verb's present participle.

For Example:

Visualize a team, three months deep into a project, their efforts ongoing until completion. This continuous journey is the realm of the Past Perfect Continuous.

Imagine a reader, immersed in a book over two weeks, a continuous engagement with the story until its return.

2. Illustrative Scenarios: Comparing Through Examples

Let's bring these tenses to life with specific scenarios:

Scene One:

Past Perfect: Envision birds having completed their journey south before winter's onset.

Past Perfect Continuous: Now, imagine these birds in the act of flying south over several days, their migration concluding with the arrival of winter.

Scene Two:

Past Perfect: A writer completes three novels before celebrating thirty years of life.

Past Perfect Continuous: Alternatively, this writer spends years in the craft of novel writing, a continuous endeavor culminating before the thirtieth birthday.

3. The Tenses in Action: Context and Usage
Emphasizing Completion vs. Duration

Past Perfect: This tense is akin to a snapshot, capturing the completion of an action.
Past Perfect Continuous: Think of this as a movie, highlighting the length and progression of an action.
Contextual Use

Past Perfect: Ideal for sequential storytelling.
Past Perfect Continuous: Perfect for setting the stage and providing a backstory.
4. The Tenses in Real Life: Writing and Speaking
These tenses transcend theory, finding their place in the practical world of communication.

In Writing: The Past Perfect sets a timeline of events, while the Past Perfect Continuous adds depth, showing actions unfolding over time.
In Speech: These tenses clarify the timing of past events, enriching our spoken narratives.
5. Tense Mastery through Practice
Exercise 1:
Transform the given sentences:

Convert a scene of someone watching a show for an hour into Past Perfect.
Turn the completion of a project before a deadline into Past Perfect Continuous.
Exercise 2:
Analyze and identify the tense:

A concert has started by the time someone arrives.
A journey of driving all night concludes with reaching a destination.
6. Embarking on a Continuous Learning Journey
Mastering these tenses is a gateway to refined communication, adding precision and depth to your language skills. To further enhance your grasp, immerse yourself in

grammar books, partake in writing exercises, and join language workshops.

Remember, mastering a language is a voyage, not a destination. Embrace the journey, continuously enriching your understanding of the English language's beautiful complexities.

This tense combines the past perfect (had) with the present participle (-ing form) to express the duration of an action that was ongoing in the past and was completed before another event occurred. To deepen your understanding of this tense, let's explore its structure, usage, and some creative examples and exercises.

Structure of Past Perfect Continuous Tense
Affirmative Form: Subject + had + been + present participle (verb + -ing).

Example: She had been waiting for three hours before the train arrived.
Negative Form: Subject + had + not + been + present participle.

Example: They had not been studying for long when the power cut happened.
Interrogative Form: Had + subject + been + present participle?

Example: Had he been working out before he joined the marathon?
Usage and Functions
To Indicate Duration Before Something in the Past: It emphasizes how long an action had been happening before another event.

Example: I had been reading the book for a month before I finally finished it.

To Show Cause and Effect: It can indicate that a past action (continuing for some time) had an effect on another event.

Example: He was exhausted because he had been running.
Creative Examples and Exercises
Exercise 1: Complete the Sentences

Jane _____ (cook) all afternoon, so she was too tired to go out in the evening.
They _____ (not play) football for long when it started to rain heavily.
How long _____ (you, work) on the project before the manager approved it?
Answers

had been cooking
had not been playing
had you been working
Exercise 2: Form Questions
Turn the following statements into questions using the past perfect continuous tense.

She had been writing her novel for two years before getting it published.
They had been traveling in Asia for months when they decided to settle in Thailand.
Answers

Had she been writing her novel for two years before getting it published?
Had they been traveling in Asia for months when they decided to settle in Thailand?
Creative Story Exercise
Write a short story using past perfect continuous tense to describe the actions of the characters before a significant event in the story.

Example Story: The Lost Necklace
Maggie had been searching for her grandmother's necklace for weeks before she finally found it in the attic. Her brother, Alex, had been helping her all this time, turning the house upside down. They had been feeling quite hopeless about finding it, as their grandmother had been quite upset about the loss. The discovery brought immense relief because they had been dreading telling their grandmother about the missing necklace.

Practical Application
Imagine a scenario in your professional or personal life where past perfect continuous tense can be appropriately used. For instance, in a workplace setting, explaining the duration of a project before its completion: "Our team had been working on the software update for several months before the successful launch."

Additional Exercises for Reinforcement
Exercise 3: Sentence Transformation
Transform these simple past tense sentences into past perfect continuous tense.

She wrote her thesis.
They traveled around Europe.
I worked on the presentation.
Answers

She had been writing her thesis for a long period before she completed it.
They had been traveling around Europe for several weeks before they returned home.
I had been working on the presentation for several hours before it was ready.
Exercise 4: Real-Life Situations
Create sentences using past perfect continuous tense based on these scenarios:

Waiting for a friend who is late.
Working on a difficult math problem.
Preparing for a marathon.
Example Sentences

I had been waiting for my friend for over an hour when she finally arrived.
He had been working on the difficult math problem all evening before he solved it.
She had been preparing for the marathon for months before the event was canceled.
By consistently practicing these exercises and applying the past perfect continuous tense in various contexts, you can enhance your understanding and usage of this intricate aspect of English grammar.

Chapter 13: The Future Perfect Continuous Tense

The Future Perfect Continuous Tense, a fascinating aspect of English grammar, represents actions that will be ongoing over a period of time and will be completed at some point in the future. This tense is particularly intriguing because it marries the concept of duration with that of completion, offering a nuanced way to express future activities.

1. Understanding the Future Perfect Continuous Tense
The structure of this tense typically includes the auxiliary verbs "will have been" followed by the present participle (the "-ing" form of the verb). The formula is: Subject + will have been + present participle + object/complement.

Examples in Practice:
By 2025, scientists will have been researching renewable energy solutions for over a decade.
She will have been working at the company for three years by the time she gets her promotion.
These examples highlight ongoing actions (researching, working) that will reach a certain point of duration by a specified time in the future (2025, time of promotion).

2. Usage in Different Contexts
The future perfect continuous tense is not as commonly used as other tenses, but it has its unique applications:

Emphasizing Duration: It's used to stress the length of time an action will have been happening up to a future moment.
Predicting Future Activities: In business or academic contexts, this tense can project future progress or achievements.
Creating Suspense or Curiosity: In storytelling, it can create a sense of anticipation about what will have been happening over a period.

3. Contrast with Other Tenses

Understanding this tense becomes clearer when contrasted with others:

Future Perfect Simple: This tense emphasizes the completion of the action by a certain time, not the duration. E.g., "She will have finished the project by next week."

Present Continuous: This tense is for ongoing actions but doesn't imply future completion. E.g., "She is working on a project."

4. Common Mistakes and Misunderstandings

Overuse: It's often overused where simpler tenses would suffice.

Confusing with Other Future Tenses: Misunderstanding its unique purpose can lead to confusion with other future forms.

5. Practical Applications

Academic Writing: Useful for expressing ongoing research or long-term studies.

Professional Settings: In business, it can articulate long-term project goals or career progressions.

6. Sample Exercises

Exercise 1: Identifying the Tense

Choose the correct tense for each sentence:

By 2030, we (a) will have been implementing (b) will implement sustainable practices for 15 years.

She (a) will have been working (b) works here until she retires next year.

Exercise 2: Correct the Sentences

Rewrite these sentences using the future perfect continuous tense:

He will complete working on the project for five years by 2024.

They will research in this field for a decade by next year.

7. Conclusion

The future perfect continuous tense, while specific in its use, provides a rich and detailed way to convey future actions with an emphasis on their duration and ongoing nature. Its understanding and correct application can greatly enhance the depth and clarity of both spoken and written English.

8. Solving the Exercises
Exercise 1: Answers
(a) will have been implementing
(a) will have been working
Exercise 2: Answers
He will have been working on the project for five years by 2024.
They will have been researching in this field for a decade by next year.
This exploration of the future perfect continuous tense demonstrates its unique role in English grammar, allowing for expressive and detailed communication about future activities and their duration.

Understanding and mastering the Future Perfect Continuous tense can be a fascinating journey into the intricacies of English grammar. This tense is used to express an action that will have been continuing up to a certain point in the future. Let's delve into the formation of affirmative, negative, and interrogative sentences in this tense.

Affirmative Sentences in Future Perfect Continuous Tense
Affirmative sentences in the Future Perfect Continuous tense are structured to indicate that an action will have been ongoing for a specified duration by a certain time in the future. The formula for forming such sentences is:

Subject + will have been + present participle (verb-ing) + for/since + time.

Examples and Explanation:
"She will have been working on the project for three hours by noon tomorrow."

Here, 'she' is the subject.
'Will have been working' is the future perfect continuous verb phrase.
'For three hours' indicates the duration.
'By noon tomorrow' specifies the future time point.
"The trees will have been growing for a decade by 2025."

'The trees' are the subject.
'Will have been growing' is the verb phrase.
'For a decade' signifies the duration.
'By 2025' marks the future time.
Negative Sentences in Future Perfect Continuous Tense
Negative sentences in this tense convey that an action will not have been continuing up to a certain point in the future. The structure is:

Subject + will not have been + present participle + for/since + time.

Examples and Explanation:
"They will not have been living here for a year by next month."

'They' is the subject.
'Will not have been living' is the verb phrase, negated with 'not'.
'For a year' indicates duration.
'By next month' is the future time point.

'I' is the subject.
'Will not have been studying' is the verb phrase.
'For more than two hours' shows duration.
'By tonight' specifies when in the future.
Interrogative Sentences in Future Perfect Continuous Tense
Interrogative sentences in this tense are used to ask about the duration of an action up to a future point. The structure is:

Will + subject + have been + present participle + for/since + time?

Examples and Explanation:
"Will you have been working at the company for ten years by 2030?"

'Will you' begins the question.
'Have been working' is the verb phrase.
'At the company' specifies the action's location.
'For ten years' indicates duration.
'By 2030' marks the future time.
"Will it have been raining for several hours by the time we leave?"

'Will it' starts the interrogative.
'Have been raining' is the verb phrase.
'For several hours' shows duration.
'By the time we leave' specifies the future time point.
Practical Applications and Exercises
Understanding this tense has real-world applications, such as in project planning, forecasting, and expressing long-term goals. It can be particularly useful in professional settings where detailed time management and future projections are essential.

Exercise 1:
Create an affirmative sentence.

Subject: The committee
Action: Discussing the proposal
Duration: Five hours
Future Time Point: By next week's meeting

Exercise 2:
Form a negative sentence.

Subject: The train
Action: Running
Duration: Eight hours
Future Time Point: By 9 AM tomorrow

Exercise 3:
Construct an interrogative sentence.

Subject: We
Action: Studying for the exam
Duration: Four hours
Future Time Point: By midnight
Answer:
"Will we have been studying for the exam for four hours by midnight?"

Concluding Thoughts
The Future Perfect Continuous tense, while complex, offers a nuanced way to express duration and continuity of actions into the future. Its mastery can enrich your communication skills, especially in scenarios requiring detailed time-related descriptions. Practice regularly, and you will find it increasingly natural to use this tense effectively.

The future perfect continuous tense, also known as the future perfect progressive, is an intriguing and nuanced aspect of English grammar. It's used to express actions that will have been ongoing over a period of time and will continue up to a specific point in the future. This tense provides a sense of duration to actions and is often employed for predictions about ongoing activities. Understanding and using this tense effectively can add depth and precision to your communication.

1. Structure and Formation of the Future Perfect Continuous Tense
The future perfect continuous tense is formed using the following structure:

Subject + will have been + present participle (verb + ing)
For example:

"By next year, I will have been working at the company for five years."

This sentence suggests that at a specific time in the future (next year), the action of working (at the company) will have continued for a certain duration (five years).

2. Expressing Duration of Actions
The future perfect continuous is particularly useful when emphasizing the duration of an action that will continue up to a certain future point. It often answers the question, "How long will something have been happening by a certain time?"

For instance:

"In December, she will have been teaching at the university for ten years."
Here, the focus is on the length of time (ten years) that she will have been engaged in the action (teaching) by a specific future moment (December).

3. Making Predictions About Ongoing Actions
This tense is also used to make predictions or guesses about what will be happening in the future, especially when these predictions are based on current trends or ongoing actions.

Example:

This sentence predicts that an ongoing action (playing football) will have reached a certain duration (over an hour) by the time a future event occurs (our arrival).

4. Practical Applications in Various Fields
In professional settings, such as project management, this tense can be invaluable for planning and forecasting. For example, a project manager might say, "By the end of the quarter, we will have been working on the project for three months." This not only communicates the timeline but also emphasizes the ongoing effort and investment in the project.

5. Sample Exercises

Exercise 1:

Fill in the blanks with the correct form of the future perfect continuous tense.

a. By 2025, I _____ (study) Spanish for 10 years.
b. They _____ (travel) for 24 hours straight by the time they reach Australia.

Answers:
a. will have been studying
b. will have been traveling

Exercise 2:

Create sentences using the future perfect continuous tense based on the given cues.

a. (finish / project / two months)
b. (live / abroad / five years)

Sample Answers:
a. "In two months, we will have been finishing the project."

6. Conclusion

In conclusion, the future perfect continuous tense is a sophisticated tool in the English language. It allows speakers to articulate actions that will be ongoing until a specific future time, emphasizing both the continuity and the duration of these actions. Its application ranges from everyday conversation to complex professional scenarios, making it a valuable aspect of effective communication. By mastering this tense, you can express temporal nuances with greater clarity and precision, enhancing both your spoken and written English.

Understanding the nuances of the English language, especially when it comes to tenses, is a fascinating and intricate aspect of linguistics. The future perfect continuous and future perfect tenses are two such intriguing aspects. In this exploration, we'll delve deeply into their differences, usage, and subtleties, providing unique insights and practical examples along the way.

Future Perfect Tense
Definition and Structure: The future perfect tense is used to describe an action that will be completed by a specific time in the future.

Usage: This tense is often used to emphasize that something will be finished before a certain point in the future.

Time Frame: The focus here is on the completion of the action. The exact duration is not important, just the fact that it will be finished.

Examples in Context:

Planning: "We will have finalized the project before the deadline."
Future Perfect Continuous Tense
Definition and Structure: This tense is used to express an action that will be ongoing until a certain point in the future. It's formed with "will have been" followed by the present participle (verb+ing).

Usage: It emphasizes the duration of an activity leading up to a specific future time.

Time Frame: The focus is on the continuous nature and the duration of the action, rather than its completion.

Examples in Context:

Continuity: "They will have been living in that house for a decade by next year."
Comparative Analysis
Completion vs. Continuation: The future perfect tense is about the completion of an action, whereas the future perfect

continuous emphasizes the ongoing nature of an action over a period leading up to a certain point.

Duration Focus: The continuous form focuses more on the process and duration, while the perfect tense emphasizes the result or the fact of completion.

Contextual Application: In practical terms, you would use the future perfect to highlight achievements or milestones, while the future perfect continuous would be more appropriate for activities that are notable for their ongoing nature.

Practical Applications and Examples
In Professional Scenarios:

Future Perfect: "We will have reached our sales target by the end of the quarter."
Future Perfect Continuous: "By next week, I will have been practicing piano for two years."
Exercises for Deeper Understanding
Identify the Tense: Read a paragraph and identify if the sentences use future perfect or future perfect continuous tense.
Rewrite the Sentence: Take a sentence in the future perfect tense and rewrite it in the future perfect continuous tense, and vice versa.
Scenario-Based Application: Create a scenario and use both tenses to describe different aspects of the situation.
Sample Exercise
Scenario: Preparing for a Marathon

Future Perfect: "By the day of the marathon, I will have trained for six months."
Future Perfect Continuous: "On the morning of the marathon, I will have been tapering my training for two weeks."

Exercise: Rewrite the above sentences, swapping the tenses.

Conclusion
The future perfect and future perfect continuous tenses, though similar in some respects, serve different purposes in conveying the nuances of time and action in the English language. By understanding these differences and practicing their usage, one can greatly enhance their linguistic precision and effectiveness, whether in professional or personal communication. As with any aspect of language, the key to mastery lies in thoughtful practice and application.

Understanding and mastering the future perfect continuous tense in English can be a rewarding challenge. This tense is used to describe an action that will have been continuing up to a point in the future. Here, we will explore this tense in depth, providing examples and exercises to enhance your grasp of its usage.

Understanding Future Perfect Continuous Tense
Structure: It generally follows the structure:

Positive: will have been + present participle (verb-ing)
Negative: will not have been + present participle
Question: Will + subject + have been + present participle?
Usage: It is used to:

Emphasize the duration of an action that will continue up to a certain point in the future.
Express the cause of a future event.
Describe an ongoing future action over a period of time.
Examples
By next year, she will have been working at the company for a decade.

This sentence emphasizes the duration of her employment.
By the time you arrive, I will have been preparing dinner for an hour.

This stresses the ongoing action of preparing dinner before your arrival.
They will not have been living in Paris for more than two years when they move again.

Here, the sentence describes a future condition that is limited by time.
Will you have been studying for your exams for three weeks by the time they start?

This question is inquiring about the duration of the studying period.

Exercises

Exercise 1: Complete the Sentences

Fill in the blanks with the correct form of the future perfect continuous tense.

By 2025, they (to work) _____ in their field for over a decade.

When you graduate, how long (you, to study) _____ at the university?

I (not, to live) _____ in this city for more than two years by the time I leave.

By the time we meet again, we (to be) _____ friends for exactly 15 years.

Exercise 2: Correct the Errors

Identify and correct the errors in the use of the future perfect continuous tense.

By next month, I will have been start my new job for two weeks.

She will not has been living here for three years by December.

Will they have been worked on the project for over a year by its completion?

Exercise 3: Create Your Own Sentences

Write sentences using the future perfect continuous tense based on these prompts:

A student studying for exams (duration: 2 months)
A family planning a vacation (duration: since last summer)
An athlete training for a marathon (duration: 6 months)
Solutions

Exercise 1:

By 2025, they will have been working in their field for over a decade.
When you graduate, how long will you have been studying at the university?
I will not have been living in this city for more than two years by the time I leave.
By the time we meet again, we will have been friends for exactly 15 years.
Exercise 2:

Corrected: By next month, I will have been starting my new job for two weeks.
Corrected: She will not have been living here for three years by December.
Corrected: Will they have been working on the project for over a year by its completion?
Exercise 3: Sample Answers

By the end of next month, I will have been studying for my exams for two months.
By next summer, we will have been planning our vacation since last summer.
In April, she will have been training for the marathon for six months.
These exercises provide a practical way to apply the future perfect continuous tense in various contexts. By practicing these exercises, you can enhance your understanding and use of this tense in both written and spoken English.

9 798223 918752